# I Believe in a God Who is Growing

*Process Perspectives on
the Creed, the Sacraments,
and the Christian Life*

BY
JOHN R. MABRY

the apocryphile press
BERKELEY, CA
www.apocryphile.org

OTHER BOOKS
BY JOHN R. MABRY

The Way of Thomas:
Nine Insights for Enlightened Living
from the Secret Sayings of Jesus

The Monster God:
Images of Horrific Divinity
in the Religions of the World

Noticing the Divine:
An Introduction to Interfaith Spiritual Guidance

Faith Styles: The Ways People Believe

God is a Great Underground River

Crisis and Communion:
The Re-Mythologization of the Eucharist

Heretics, Mystics & Misfits

God As Nature Sees God:
A Christian Reading of the Tao Te Ching

The Tao Te Ching:
A New Translation

The Little Book of the Tao Te Ching

# I Believe
# in a God
# Who is Growing

apocryphile press
BERKELEY, CA


Apocryphile Press
1700 Shattuck Ave #81
Berkeley, CA 94709
www.apocryphile.org

Cover art by Gina Rose Halpern,
used by permission.
Illustrations by Brian Zampier, used by permission.

This book is dedicated to
the people of Grace North Church,
to whom these sermons were delivered,
and especially to the memory of

ROYAL THOMPSON

who served us so well for so long.

# Contents

PART ONE:       WHY PROCESS THOUGHT?

CHAPTER ONE     *A Reasonable Faith*......................11
CHAPTER TWO     *Why I Don't Like Models*
*Well, Okay, I Do Like*
*Some Models*.................................23

PART TWO:       THE APOSTLES' CREED

CHAPTER THREE *I Believe in God, the Father,*
*the Almighty, Creator of*
*Heaven and Earth* ........................35
CHAPTER FOUR *I Believe in Jesus Christ, his*
*only Son, our Lord. He was*
*conceived by the power of*
*the Holy Spirit, and born*
*of the Virgin Mary*........................43
CHAPTER FIVE   *He suffered under Pontius Pilate,*
*was crucified, dead, and buried.*
*He descended into hell.*
*On the third day he rose again.*
*He ascended into heaven,*
*and is seated at the right hand*
*of the Father. He will come*
*again to judge the living and*
*the dead*.......................................55

CHAPTER SIX        *I believe in the Holy Spirit,* ...........67
CHAPTER SEVEN  *the holy catholic Church,*
                            *the Communion of Saints,* ..............79
CHAPTER EIGHT   *the forgiveness of sins,* ...................89
CHAPTER NINE     *the resurrection of the body,*
                            *and the life everlasting. Amen.* ...101

PART THREE: THE SACRAMENTS

CHAPTER TEN            *Baptism* ...........................117
CHAPTER ELEVEN      *Confirmation* ...................129
CHAPTER TWELVE     *Eucharist* ........................137
CHAPTER THIRTEEN  *Marriage* .......................145
CHAPTER FOURTEEN *Ordination* ........................155
CHAPTER FIFTEEN     *Confession* ........................165
CHAPTER SIXTEEN    *Unction* ...........................173

PART FOUR: BEING CHRISTIAN, BEING REAL

CHAPTER SEVENTEEN *Do Justice* ........................189
CHAPTER EIGHTEEN   *Love Kindness.* ..................195
CHAPTER NINETEEN   *Walk Humbly*
                              *with Your God* .................205

# PART ONE

# Why Process Thought?

*All wisdom is from the Holy One,*
*and with God it remains forever.*

Ecclesiasticus 1:1

# Chapter One

## *A Reasonable Faith*

Christians today face challenges undreamt of by our forbears. In ages past, the universe could be described in terms of the laws of physics, and God was on his throne in heaven. There were certain things you could put your faith in, things that were sure. Scripture could be counted on as an indisputable authority, and Mother Church could put all our fears to rest.

It is not so today. It is almost impossible to find someone who is completely trusting of church leaders or institutions. It is difficult to reconcile the claims of historic Christianity with the realities and paradoxes posed by physics and philosophy, and few people feel up to the task of even trying.

I have been tempted to give up on Christianity and the Church. And like many people, I have been wounded by fundamentalism, offended by pious dogmatism, and profoundly challenged in my efforts to reconcile sense and spirit in my own life. My own journey has been long and circuitous, spiraling in and out of faith, oscillating between questioning and finding.

Once, as my former spouse and I were cleaning the garage, Kate came across a box of old journals. Of course, she couldn't resist digging in right then and there, finding a few choice things to read aloud and to be embarrassed about. After a couple of nuggets of good cringe-material, she opened one of the journals to a particularly poignant spot: to an account of the night we met.

It was six years ago, in a Denny's restaurant. I had been running a Fundamentalists Anonymous group for people recovering from abusive religious experience, and Kate saw my ad in the newspaper. She had been raised as a fundamentalist evangelical and had suffered under that oppressive system every bit as much as I.

It was a good meeting; one that I remember well. I mostly talked; Kate mostly cried; and her journal's account bore all this out. But then she read something which I had all but forgotten about. I had, at that time, reached a conclusion that there were three doctrines I could wholeheartedly embrace; about all else, I was agnostic. I have, in the intervening years, almost completely forgotten about my three hard-won doctrines, but Kate not only remembered them from one telling, but she recorded them in her journal.

The three doctrines are these:

Number one: You cannot know. Religious traditions represent our "best guesses." When we are honest with ourselves, we must admit that *we can not know.*

The second doctrine is: religion motivated by fear is invalid.

The third doctrine is similar to the second: religion motivated by personal salvation is immoral.

I'm not really going to elaborate much on these, but hearing them after so many years, I am struck by how indicative they are of my generation. At midlife, I am on the cusp of what popular culture has named Generation X, those who missed out on the idealism of the 60s and were given no suitable ideology to take its place. Generation Xers are cynical, suspicious, and largely pessimistic about the world in general. My doctrines represent in a distilled form the attitudes of many young people. You cannot know. I will not allow you to manipulate me by fear. Nor will I buy into the lie that the part is more important than the whole.

These are not attitudes that could have existed in ages past. They are the product of Post-modernity, a time when all of our cherished ideas about how the universe functions have been blown away by quantum mechanics, when all of our ideas about God have been reduced to the evolution of human consciousness, when any scriptures we once held as sacred have been deconstructed and dissected into contradictory and non-authoritative layers of text.

These attitudes are born out of a scientific world-view, of which most people have chosen to simply live in denial, a worldview that says that all symbol systems and all cultural markers are arbitrary and vacant of any intrinsic meaning or value. This worldview is deeply distrustful of corporations and hierarchy, and sees that our personal greed and Machiavellian attitudes towards the planet may have already rung the death-knell for succeeding generations.

This worldview is not a bad thing, in my opinion. Yes, it's uncomfortable and unsettling, but it is also part of the painful process of the human race growing out of adolescence into adulthood. I neither scorn nor struggle against the time I was born into; instead, I endeavor to struggle *with* it.

After one has taken in all that post-modernity implies, it is difficult to reconcile oneself to the pat, black-and-white answers of a catechism. Several years ago I began to ask myself questions about what one *can* affirm in the Christian tradition. I began to look for something concrete, something that would answer the question: if all of our signposts have been taken away, how are we to make sense of this tradition? If the formulations of past generations seem senseless today, how do we make them sensible?

I believe that we can learn a lot by understanding how the beliefs and teachings which make up Christianity were understood in their own times, in their own cultures. If we understood the problems faced by our ancestors, if we knew the questions they were asking, we might see more clearly why they answered as they did. We may also then understand why the answers they gave may or may not be appropriate for us now.

## Making Sense

A while back I heard a story about a young boy who came home from Sunday School, and when asked what he had learned, answered that he had learned God's name: Harold. The parents were initially upset until, upon further questioning, they discovered that the boy had also learned the Lord's Prayer, which he rendered, "Our Father, which art in heaven, Harold be thy name..."

Now this boy was doing what we all do: making sense of the world in terms of what we know. He had never heard the word "hallowed" before, so he grasped on to a word which he did know that sounded mighty close and seemed to make a lot of sense. And like that little boy, we grown-ups have always tried to understand God, the unknowable, in terms of the familiar.

Throughout history, we have tried to make sense of God, the universe, and our place in it as best we could, with the help of the most up-to-date philosophies and ideas. So even though Christians in the first century and Christians in the third century honored the same scriptures and repeated the same words when they recited the Apostles' Creed, they understood their meanings in vastly different ways. One could say the same for a Roman Catholic Christian of the ninth century or a German Protestant Christian of the seventeenth century. Each of them repeated the same formulas, but the ideas behind them were worlds apart.

This is because theology is an ever-evolving phenomenon. The Jews even have a term for it, "Midrash," the ongoing interpretation, or even revelation, of Scripture developing in collaboration with everyday human experience.

Christians are intimately familiar with this process. Take the history of the Apostles' Creed, for instance— this is a story that takes three centuries to tell, as it changed and evolved into the familiar text we know today.

The earliest Christians, of course, had no need to outline a coherent theology. They had first-hand experience of these things. Words like "trinity" or "transubstantiation" would have had no meaning for them. They had a real experience with the risen Christ, and none of them had really taken all of this to its logical conclusions just yet. The apostle Paul was the first to propose the concept of the "Cosmic Christ" which indwells and sustains the whole of Creation, but I'm not sure all of the apostles would have been sold on Paul's Neo-Platonic recasting of what had happened to them. But he was writing for pagans and had to appeal to them as intellectual equals, and on their turf.

Many Christians of the second through the fourth centuries continued in Paul's footsteps, including such noted authorities as Panteanus, Clement of Alexandria, Pseudo-Dionysus and Origen, some of the greatest theologians of the early church. Most of them were Neo-platonists before their conversions, so naturally they explained their faith in terms of their Platonic worldview. The result was that in Antiquity Christian thought became a force to be reckoned with.

Later, when medieval Europe rediscovered Aristotle through Arabic translations, and scholars of the Western world seized upon Aristotle's refutation of the Platonic world-view, St. Thomas Aquinas would, in his voluminous writings, create an Aristotelian systematic theology that satisfied the philosophical wrestlings of his age.

During the Reformation, the reformers demanded that their faith be rational and banished anything smacking of priestcraft or superstition. The Congregationalists were at the forefront of political philosophy by insisting that the community of God be democratic and egalitarian. And in recent times, many Christian thinkers see their faith as congruent with such contemporary philosophical perspectives as Process Thought and Systems Theory.

In each age we have all said, "I believe in God..." but our images and ideas regarding the actual *meaning* of those words have often been quite different.

I searched for many years to discover a world-view I could put my faith in. I embraced what science taught me as just more information about God. There is not for me—and for many Christians—any conflict between science and biblical faith, perhaps because we don't approach either one of them uncritically.

We know that what science tells us today might be changed by a scientific discovery that happens tomorrow—that's just science evolving. And we know just as well that we should not start executing football teams just because the Torah says that we should put to death anyone that touches the skin of a dead pig. That's just theology evolving.

It seems most natural that as our species evolves, our ideas about God evolve. Archeological research shows that our earliest ancestors thought of the divine only as mischievous spirits hiding in the woods. As time went on, the "spirits" got bigger, and took on the gigantic proportions of the Hindu, Greek and Nordic pantheons. The Abrahamic inspiration and Upanishadic Hinduism are parallel epiphanies which saw all the "regional" gods as really pointing to one, great "universal" god, the One God.

But God's evolution did not stop there. The early Israelite's experience of God was that "he" was a capricious and often childish personality, a god with good intentions but often devious means. The prophets often called God on "his" behavior, and the God of the later prophets calls us to a more refined understanding of community and justice.

Jesus stands in this tradition, as one who has wrestled with God, and through whose wrestling both God and humankind were changed forever.

Jesus did not see himself as breaking from tradition—instead he saw tradition as something that should serve people, not the other way around, and so pushed the boundaries of his tradition much more than the religious authorities were comfortable with. Through Jesus' attention to human experience and human need, he made his faith relevant to the people around him.

Although it took a long time, Christians eventually came to realize that this was Jesus' genius. The idea that "experience" was important as a conscious guide to faith was long buried. For the first fifteen hundred years of the church we relied on the twin pillars of scripture and tradition, and afforded them equal weight. The Reformers discarded tradition and relied on the single pillar, *sola scriptura*, proclaiming Scripture as their only authority. The Church of England, however, embraced a "middle path." In congruence with the rationalism of the time they honored tradition, scripture, and reason as having equal weight in deciding matters of faith. But it wasn't until John Wesley, the founder of Methodism, that we have a significant number of Christians embracing the "Wesleyan Quadrilateral" of tradition, scripture, reason, and experience. It seems a shame that Jesus' own approach to faith should be so long ignored!

The re-invention of the faith outlined above progressed whether or not Christians embraced the principle that it *should* progress. It is always going to go on, so long as Christians seek to be credible members of both their historical faith and their contemporary world. So it is fitting to try to understand the Apostles' Creed, this most basic statement of our common faith, in terms philosophically relevant for people in our time.

This book is offered in the hope that these ancient words which have guided the church for centuries might be vibrant and alive for us today, so that we may without shame affirm our faith in God as we have come to know God, and still be credible witnesses in this universe as we have come to know the universe.

Process Theology has been very popular in the last thirty years precisely because it provides a conceptual model which can reconcile faith and science. This kind of model is frequently called a world-view or a "paradigm." One would be hard-pressed to find a seminary in any major denomination in the West, from Roman Catholic to Southern Baptist, that does not cover the Process model as a way of understanding the Christian faith.

So why is it that we do not hear the insights of Process Theology preached from the pulpit? Well, although most pastors have had to study Process Theology, they rarely preach about it overtly, since it is kind of technical and difficult to describe. This is unfortunate, as Alfred North Whitehead, Charles Heartshorne, John Cobb, and many others have elucidated a way of seeing the universe that resolves many philosophical dilemmas in light of quantum research and systems theory, as well as solving many theological problems.

The difficulty is that Process Theology requires a radical shift of perspective in our understanding of time, and in order to speak of it properly, these thinkers have had to invent a vocabulary that is difficult to translate into regular street terminology. The result is that Process Theology remains the domain of scientists, philosophers, theology professors, and pastors. Rarely does it seep out into the pews.

As a person for whom Process Thought has done a great deal in unifying my worldview, I find this to be a tragic situation. I do not consider myself more intelligent than the average person, and so I have no doubt that these insights might be valuable to just about anybody.

I have heard many Episcopalians say that if you can get to the place where you can say the Creed with a straight face, you'll be all right. I agree, but I don't think it has to be such an arduous journey. There are Christian thinkers who are on the forefront of Systems philosophy, and there is no reason for us to each individually reinvent the wheel. Thus I have undertaken in this book a serious and hopefully enlightening look at the most basic tenants of our faith in light of our knowledge and culture as twenty-first century Christians.

We are going to walk through our faith, element by element, revisiting the words of the Creed spoken by Christians the world over for two millennia. We will ask what they mean to us as post-modern people. And we are going to have to stretch some, conceptually. Getting the hang of the Process worldview is a bit like riding a unicycle. It's *similar* to riding a bicycle, but there's a whole other element to it that has to come first or you'll hit the pavement. In the next chapter we'll talk about the evolution of the Creed and the 180 degree twist required of our brains by Process Thought.

*God of surprise and change,*
*From our perspective it seems*
*that in some ways we have grown up together.*
*Hold us safe in your wise embrace,*
*teach us not to be afraid to use our imaginations,*
*to face with courage the questions put to us by*
*the sages of our time.*
*Assure us that as a loving parent*
*you will cling to us into whatever world we venture.*
*Encourage us by showing us that the gospel is larger*
*than the culture that contains it.*
*Comfort us by your Holy Spirit*
*with the certain knowledge*
*that we are sealed and anointed*
*as Christ's own forever. Amen.*

*When I look at your heavens, the work of your fingers,*
*the moon and the stars that you have established;*
*what are human beings*
*that you are mindful of them;*
*mortals, that you care for them?*

Psalm 8:3

# Chapter Two

## Why I Don't Like Models . . .
## Well, Okay, I Do Like Some Models

W hen I was a little boy, I wasn't much different in my tastes from others my age. I spent most of my time collecting matchbox cars and playing cowboys and Indians. One pastime which I always felt I should get into but never seemed to quite crack was model-building. I would gawk and gasp at the models my friends had constructed, mostly with help from their dads. Mainly they were model cars, exquisitely detailed and fully loaded, with lots of shiny chrome and tan plastic simulated leather interiors. Cool.

The problem was I just didn't have the patience for such undertakings. I have infinite patience for things I consider worthwhile, and though I admired the models my friends had painstakingly built, I am such a guilt-driven person that it is hard for me to do something which I suspect is just "wasting time." The problem with building models, then, was that I was very aware that they weren't real cars. With a real car I could understand putting in so much precious time. But these were models, and as such, I simply couldn't justify it.

I feel lucky, because I think that sometimes people have difficulty distinguishing models from reality. We get an idea into our head of how something is supposed to be, and then we live in denial if the reality our ideas supposedly describe doesn't fit. The Buddha used a now famous analogy to illustrate this point. "The Dharma (my teaching)" he said, "is just a finger pointing to the moon. Don't confuse the finger with the moon." Likewise models, from model cars to model cosmologies, are just that: pointers to that which they represent. They are not themselves the reality.

Now, having made this distinction, perhaps it is safe to introduce the two models I would like to discuss in this chapter: the Apostles' Creed and Process Theology. Neither of these can be taken as gospel truth—but they both point to truth, and if we look closely we might be able to catch a glimpse of the moon that they both indicate.

The Apostles' Creed is perhaps one of the oldest—and certainly one of the most influential—documents of the early church. Like most things from this period, it is steeped in folklore. It gets its name from a legend which says that before the apostles went their different ways to preach the gospel, they decided to create a normative outline of the faith, so that they could be sure they were all teaching the same things. The legend says that each apostle is responsible for one of the clauses in the Creed.

This is a wonderful piece of folklore, but, I fear, dreadful church history. Most historians agree that it has its origins in the baptismal formula that developed in the early church, a formula that continues to be in use to this day. Those about to be baptized were asked a series of questions about what they believed, and the correct answers, standardized later into the liturgy, formed the basis of the document so familiar to us.

It is not the only creed, of course. Several were kicking around during the first few centuries, such as the Jerusalem Creed and the Old Roman Creed, of which it is an elaboration. It is first found in its present form in the early eighth century. The Apostles' Creed has also been overshadowed in liturgical usage by the Nicene Creed, ratified in 381. The Nicene Creed was consciously constructed and implemented, whereas the Apostles' and its predecessor creeds arose organically out of the baptismal rites, and its usage spread only because of its popularity. St. Athanasius' Creed is also famous, but it is difficult to read, even in English, and is rarely used liturgically.

None of the other creeds, however, demonstrate the concise elegance and popularity amongst common people as the Apostles' Creed, and it is this document that has provided the church, officially or no, with the standard against which orthodoxy could be judged for nearly two thousand years.

It is, I would like to remind you, a model. It is not divinely-inspired scripture. It did not drop whole from heaven. But it does point to truths witnessed to by Christians down through the ages, and can be said by all Christians, from Catholics to Pentecostals, to be a guiding statement of Christian faith.

But as we saw in the first chapter, how people have understood this faith and how they have interpreted the words of the Creed have differed greatly, as Christians have sought to make sense of these basic elements of Christianity in terms of the philosophical models *en vogue* in their times. And this brings us to the second of the two models I would like to discuss: Process Thought.

The earliest of the "Process thinkers" was Heraclitus, who told us that you can never step into the same river twice, because when you go to step into it the second time, the water which constituted the river when you first stepped in is long gone, replaced by completely new water, thus making it a completely different river.

Heraclitus helped us to see that there are no static objects in the universe; all is in "flux," in motion. In the early twentieth century, the famous mathematician Alfred North Whitehead took this idea further. He believed that static, objective matter is an illusion of the Western imagination. The reality is harder to pin down, messier, and far more glorious. Matter and time cannot be divorced, and we can only talk about one in terms of the other. In Whitehead's view, there are no static moments, all is moving in four dimensions at all times; all is in flux; all is in the process of changing from one state to another; all is in the process of "becoming" other than it is.

There is no choice: time marches relentlessly onward. Any illusions of permanence or security are just that—illusions. All of reality is in a constant state of "becoming," in process toward the fulfillment of its potentialities.

This is no mere philosophy. Whitehead's thought is

perfectly congruent with many of the paradoxical situations posed by quantum mechanics and is, in fact, supported by them. Newtonian physics was thrown into crisis when, in the twentieth century, it was discovered that at the very smallest measurable subatomic level, there is no mass, only action—only the leaping in and out of the void of unpredictible motions of energy.

Whitehead is also aided in his thinking by the philosophy of Hegel, who believed that nothing is an island, that all is interconnected. Indeed, all things are merely "parts" of a much greater "whole," or as he put it: "Philosophy is concerned with the true, and the true is the whole" (Hegel, quoted in Copleston, Frederick, SJ, *A History of Philosophy, Vol. VII* [New York: Doubleday, 1965], p. 170).

In Whitehead's (and Hegel's) philosophy, God and the universe are a single organism. The universe is the "body" of God in a way. The great medieval Christian mystic Meister Eckhart shared this view and wrote, "God created all things in such a way that they are not outside himself" (Fox, Matthew, OP, ed. *Meditations with Meister Eckhart [Santa Fe: Bear & Co., 1983], p. 22*). Every thing that is, then, is in God. Or rather, everything that is, is growing, changing, dying, and being reborn within the ever-changing, ever-evolving body of God.

Modern physics also supports this view. The cutting edge of cosmology is Systems Theory, which posits a self-organizing principle behind the universe. A subset of this is chaos theory which detects pattern and design in random sequences. And then there is the Gaia hypothesis, which sees the earth as an organism with self-protective systems similar to those possessed by our own bodies, which some scientists believe explains otherwise inexplicable meteorological patterns, as well as behavioral changes in both humans and animals.

Whitehead preceded these advances by over fifty years, and yet Whitehead's God is unique among these systems in that, for him, God is intimate and personal. As far as Whitehead is concerned, it is not just the universe that is dependent upon God for existence. His God amazes us with his/her vulnerability, for Whitehead's God is more reciprocal and limited than we are used to thinking of God in the West. For Whitehead, God is intricately bound up in the progress of the universe. When we change, God changes, and when we grow, God grows. Thus, Whitehead can say that "it is as true to say that God creates the world as that the world creates God." The universe and God are caught up in an ongoing dance through time, inseparable, unstoppable, ever moving into new potentialities and verdant with burgeoning possibilities.

Because both Whitehead and modern physics believe the static universe to be an illusion, we are left with quite a quandary: we have no vocabulary to describe this kind of universe. A hammer is a fine tool until you try to use it to open a bottle of wine! English is simply the wrong tool for the job. Our language is noun-based: it posits static things, to which actions "happen." In Whitehead's universe, there are no "things," only "happenings," only an infinite and ever-widening spiral of actions.

The problem isn't just English, actually; none of the languages of the Indo-European language group have the capacity to describe the universe in these terms. In fact, the only known language suitable to the task is Hopi! And Hopi Process theologians are a rare breed, indeed.

To counter this, Whitehead has had to invent several new terms in order to try to talk about his ideas coherently. Thankfully, I'm only going to tell you about a couple of the most important.

Whitehead refers to all things, even human beings, as "occasions." These are the basic units, the "drops of experience," the "final real things of which the world is made." Everything that is is an occasion, from an amoeba to God. Everything that can be experienced is an ongoing string of experiences unto itself, and is itself an occasion, a moment that actually exists within a certain span of time. Only things that can be measured in time have any existence. Apart from temporal existence, there is nothing. Thus, an "occasion" is a thing that exists within time, be it a rock or a human being or the Horsehead Nebula.

Another term is "Concrescence." This is analogous to the Buddhist concept of "dependent co-arising," in that the great multiplicity of occasions interrelate in such a way that a more complex unity results. This is how little occasions combine to make big ones. Occasions join together, or as Whitehead says, they "concresce" into larger occasions. We see this in an atom spinning through space, being attracted to another atom to form a molecule; it also describes a boy and a girl falling in love and becoming a family.

If you are still having trouble with these concepts, try thinking about them this way: every cell in your body is full of little organisms, and every cell is an organism itself. Your body is filled with billions of organisms, and you yourself are an organism, living on the organism called the earth, which is an organism in a larger organism called the universe, which is an organism within an organism we call God. But all these organisms are changing all the time, prehending from each other and concrescing continuously in such a way that we can only speak of them as processes, not static objects. Are you with me?

This is just a very rough introduction to Process Thought, and I have deliberately refrained from talking about Whitehead's ideas about God in particular, since that is the subject of the next chapter.

I am hoping that this little introduction will get the wheels churning upstairs. At the very least, perhaps you are thinking, "How in the world is he going to bring these two together?" Which is just the sort of dramatic tension preachers and writers crave! So if that thought has crossed your mind, I am pleased.

There is a great deal of difference between the kind of models I longed to build as a child and the kinds of models we have just described. For one thing, I always thought that a well-constructed scale-model hot rod was pretty to look at, while Whitehead's model is at first glance a god-awful mess. But stick with me, and perhaps you'll see why I have a great deal more patience with Whitehead than I did with hot rods. Hot rods can brighten up a shelf in a little boy's room, but the kinds of models we are talking about here can change the world, change the course of history, and according to Whitehead, change God. At least I'm not feeling guilty that I'm wasting my time.

*Ever-changing, ever-living God,*
*in you we live and move and have our being.*
*Help us to peek out of the little prisons*
*we have built for ourselves,*
*to be open to new ways of seeing*
*ourselves and our universe.*
*Most of all help us not be afraid to ask new questions,*
*to posit new ideas, to explore new models,*
*even as we cling to those which have given us life,*
*your life in the Spirit. Amen.*

# PART TWO

# The Apostles' Creed

*Bless the Lord, all created things;*
*sing his praise and exalt him forever.*

Song of the Three Holy Children

# Chapter Three

## *I Believe in God,*
## *the Father, Almighty,*
## *Creator of Heaven and Earth.*

One of my favorite movies is an odd, extravagant film called *The Adventures of Baron Münchhausen,* in which Robin Williams, as King of the Moon, has a very difficult time keeping his head on his shoulders. His head, which quickly grows tired of his body, whizzes off into space at the slightest provocation, where it can contemplate "lofty" and worthy subjects such as philosophy while his headless body below rushes around like a chicken in a similar state greedily and mindlessly trying to sate its "carnal" desires, which usually means chasing the Queen of the Moon relentlessly until she gives up and allows him his way with her.

What director Terry Gilliam is lampooning here is the unwise separation between the mind and the body perpetrated by both Platonic philosophy and the rationalism of the enlightenment. This thread of philosophy is correct in noting that there is certainly a distinction between our mental and physical experiences, but it does us no favors by positing so absolute a distinction, as one cannot be fully human without both the mind and the body.

Nor, Process Theology teaches us, can God be fully divine without both aspects. In fact, it may be said that having these two indispensable aspects is what makes us in God's image. Process Theology calls the "mind" of God the transcendent, or "Primordial Nature" of God. God's transcendent nature confirms many of our traditional notions of God, such as consistency, immutability, dispassion; that God is the most powerful being in the universe and knows all that can be known. But this is not an exhaustive description of God's transcendent nature, for it is here, in the mind of God, that every creative notion, every spark of novelty has its origin. It is here that the infinite potentialities for the universe are held in trust, ready to inform and inspire every creature towards greater complexity, creativity, and harmony.

Enlightenment philosophy denies God's ability to act in the world, seeing all events in terms of cause and effect. The religious expression of this philosophy is deism, which posits God as a grand watchmaker who set the universe in motion and essentially disappeared. This kind of "absentee landlord" approach to God even informs the theologies of such noted thinkers as Bultmann and Bonhoeffer, who taught that although God has concern for the world, God does not intervene in any supernatural way.

But Process Theology again confirms the ancient Christian notion of God being concerned for, and an active participant in, the world, which is thought of as God's other nature, God's imminent nature. God acts in the universe, God's own body, not by miraculously suspending the laws of nature, nor by gigantic displays of natural catastrophes. According to Process Thought, God is present and concerned with every activity in the universe and influences these activities only by the power of suggestion.

In humans and many animals these "suggestions" might take the form of instincts, but they also allow us choices based on emotions and care for others. In Process Thought, God's transcendent nature "breaks in" to our consciousness through dreams, intuitions, instinct, art, and our conscience. Through these and other means God attempts to persuade us toward greater creativity and more abundant life.

It is in this way, Process Thought teaches, that God has guided the long process of evolution both on this planet and in the universe. When we say that we believe in God, "the creator of heaven and earth," we are speaking about a seventeen-billion-year history of goading the simplest of creatures to new heights of creativity, spurring them to develop into ever more complicated and harmonious beings. In this way God has painstakingly, heartbreakingly held in loving care every success and every failure on this grand experiment called "the earth." Not forcing us to grow, but luring us onward, leaving us free to decide to be creative or to simply let things be as they are.

And this is where Process Thought diverges from traditional theology. The Creed says that God is "Almighty," which is usually limited in its meaning to "omnipotence," but in the Process model, *suggestion* is the limit of God's power. That is not such a bad thing: the power to persuade all creatures is a formidable power indeed, unmatched and even unapproached by any other "occasion" or created being. Therefore Process Theology affirms "Almighty" status by affirming the supremacy of God's power relative to the power wielded by even the mightiest of creatures.

But in the Process model, God is not particularly concerned with power. Power seems to be more of a human obsession. God is much more interested in persuasion. God does not coerce, not only because God does not have the means to do so, but also because it is entirely outside of God's nature to do so. For, according to fellow NACCC member John Cobb, "Process Theology's understanding of divine love is in harmony with the insight...gain[ed] both from psychologists and from our own experience, that if we truly love others we do not seek to control them. We do not seek to pressure them with promises and threats involving extrinsic rewards and punishments. Instead we try to persuade them to actualize those possibilities which they themselves will find intrinsically rewarding" (Cobb, John & David Griffin. *Process Theology: An Introductory Exposition* [Philadelphia: The Westminster Press, 1976], p. 53).

It is the compassionate care with which God guides and instructs us that prompts Jesus and us to call God "Father," not because God is distant, removed, unemotional and powerful, or any of the other typically masculine attributes which we normally associate with God. But rather, because God is so relentlessly maternal, nurturing, compassionate, and intricately involved in the lives of all beings, we are prompted to speak of this being as a loving parent who watches out for our welfare and who wishes only the best for us. In another culture we may very well have called God mother, and indeed, many cultures have, and they are not wrong. Calling God "Father" has nothing to do with God's gender for Christians, but with how God relates to those whom God has midwifed into the world.

And it is precisely because of this "relational" attribute of God that we can say "I believe in God" at all. For if God were not an intensely personal being, we would only be able to say "I believe *that* God is such and such..." and then make all kinds of speculations about the divine nature. But that is not what the Creed says. The Creed says, "I believe *in* God..." which is a very different thing altogether. It betrays God's desire for intimacy and relationship with us, and our similar desires for God. For instance, my wife can say "I believe you," in which case I know that she is satisfied that I am telling the truth about something. But when she says, "I believe *in* you," which she has on several occasions, it is no longer a statement of fact; it is a statement of faith. When she says that, all kinds of feelings run through me that don't run through me when she simply says, "I believe you."

When she says "I believe *in* you," I feel trusted, worthwhile, and confident because someone else has confidence in me. It is a statement of great intimacy, and it is in this spirit that we speak the words of the Creed, "I believe *in* God."

It is *feeling* that I am interested in! And according to

Process Thought, feeling—emotional intensity—is one of the most important factors in the universe. As an "emotional" person, I appreciate a theology that affirms the blessedness of my feelings!

Whitehead says that all things *feel*, from God to a rock. A rock feels, or experiences, the ground upon which it rests, and when it is on the bottom of the ocean, it feels or experiences the pressure of so many tons of water pressing upon it from all sides. Likewise, for animals, humans, God, and other more complex occasions, feeling is our primary means of interacting in the world. We feel other occasions and processes through our senses, and we have feelings about what we experience, and those feelings generate actions and still more feelings.

Unlike the King of the Moon, we cannot divorce our intellect from either our feelings or our bodies, the instruments of feeling. Nor does God divorce God's transcendent nature from God's imminent nature, for the transcendent is always whispering ideas and ideals, guiding the long process of evolution and growth which is experienced in God's imminent nature, the universe. We participate in both natures, as we share both natures, making the whole of our humanness much greater than the sum of its parts.

Now if at this point you are reeling a little from this rather deep plunge into Process Thought, I would like to remind you that I do not present Process Theology as *the truth*. In the words of Patsy in *Monty Python and the Holy Grail*, "It's only a model." Process Thought is one way of understanding God. I'm asking you to try it on for size. If it doesn't fit, don't wear it. The real truth is that God is primarily Mystery. What we know about

God is pitifully little compared to what we don't know. We have many words and many ideas, but the whole is so much greater, so much more mysterious than anything that we can conceive of, that once we have exhausted our lexicons and debated all our theologies, God remains at once strangely intimate and yet ultimately unknowable, still more mystery than describable entity, forever beyond our ability to explain or even understand.

> *Oh, God, you are a mystery to us,*
> *you are beyond the power of our words to describe,*
> *or our minds to behold.*
> *Help us, even so, O God, to revel in that which you*
> *have revealed about yourself:*
> *that with your loving hand*
> *you formed the earth and all her creatures;*
> *that your concern for us is intimate and protective,*
> *as a mother's for her child;*
> *and that your desire for us is abundant life,*
> *"a good measure, pressed down, shaken together,*
> *running over," and to share this good life*
> *with the people you have led into our lives*
> *to be family and community for each other,*
> *now and always, as you are God always,*
> *Creator, Word, and Holy Spirit. Amen.*

*Christ is the image of the invisible God,*
*the firstborn of all creation;*
*for in him all things*
*in heaven and on earth*
*were created.*

Colossians 1:15

# Chapter Four

*I Believe in Jesus Christ,*
*his only Son, our Lord.*
*He was conceived by*
*the power of the Holy Spirit,*
*and born of the Virgin Mary...*

I do a lot of preaching, both in my church and in my various chaplaincies, but nearly every week as I listen to our senior pastor, Fr. Richard, I am struck by how different our styles are. Richard is brilliant at speaking extemporaneously, without notes, whereas I always write my sermons out ahead of time. In fact, I can think of nothing quite so frightening as arriving for worship with a sermon to give and finding that I have left it at home. I have nightmares about such incidents!

Well, one Saturday morning my nightmare came true when I arrived at the Guardian of Rossmoor nursing home without my sermon! Trying to make the best of it, I thought, "Heck, they can't fire me—I volunteer!" and I stood up after the Gospel to give my sermon Richard-style.

I hadn't a clue what I was going to say, unfortunately, and when I opened my mouth, the words that popped out were, "Before Jesus was born as a man, he was a woman." Needless to say, that was probably the most poorly received sermon I have ever given, and the *only* time anyone has ever walked out on a sermon of mine, to my knowledge.

Determined not to make the same mistake again, I hope that I'll be able to present the subject matter in a more digestible form in writing. Bear with me to see what I mean.

In this chapter we begin our discussion of the Apostles' Creed with the second clause, which is concerned with the person of Jesus Christ. The creed says "I believe in Jesus Christ, [God's] only Son, our Lord." Now that's a lot of names, a lot of attributes! Let's take them one at a time and see if we can sort out this enormous mess theologians call "Christology," or the study of Christ.

I call it a mess, because there are no definitive answers to a lot of questions, even for "orthodox" theologians. Some theologians separate the concept of "the Christ" from the person of Jesus of Nazareth, and some will not even entertain a distinction. In this book we will take a middle path, acknowledging a distinction between the two but denying their ultimate divorce.

Let's start with the concept of "the Christ" and work our way up to the person of Jesus of Nazareth. The word "Christ" is from the Greek "*xristos*" which means the same thing as the Hebrew "Messiah" or God's Anointed One. So just who is this anointed one?

For a complete answer to this question, we have to go back a long way. The *Gospel of John* states, "In the beginning was the Word...all things were made through him, and without him were no things made." Thus, scripture teaches us that the Christ, the Word, was "in the beginning with God" and is in fact a part of the Godhead, since St. John says, "the Word *was* God."

One might think that this is a bold Christological statement that really caused a ruckus in the ancient world, but that is not the case. The truth is that John is appealing to an already popular Greek notion of the divine Word as an ordering principle in the universe.

But at the same time, John is also alluding to the Jewish mythology of "Heokma," the Wisdom of God, "Sophia" in Greek. St. John, in the prologue to his Gospel, is recalling the book of Proverbs, in which this figure of Holy Wisdom is personified. Proverbs says "The LORD by Wisdom founded the earth." The words of John's Gospel are an intentional reflection of this verse, as John intends us to connect the person of Jesus (a *new* idea) with the figure of Holy Wisdom (a very *old* idea). This appeal to tradition, history, and popular philosophy lent authority to John's bold assertion that Holy Wisdom became flesh and dwelt among us.

This figure of Holy Wisdom in the Hebrew scriptures was a popular image, especially since it provided for the Jews a feminine aspect of God—"Heokma" is a feminine noun in Hebrew. Holy Wisdom is pictured in scripture as a gentle and wise woman who cries out in the streets and in the marketplaces, calling all who will to walk in her ways.

How did the feminine "Wisdom," you might be asking, get turned into the masculine "Word?" This was not a Christian innovation, but a Jewish one. About one hundred years BCE, Philo sought to introduce Jewish philosophical ideas to the Greek culture, and in so doing, he "translated" the old Jewish idea of "Wisdom" into the long-respected philosophical idea of the "Logos" or the "Word." Since *logos* is a masculine noun in Greek, Wisdom lost her feminine character.

The concepts of Wisdom and the Word were similar enough in the two cultures for the "translation" to "stick," since we see that over a hundred years later, St. John adopts the Greek "Word" to describe this ancient character called the Wisdom of God. Other cultures have concepts that are similar. The ancient idea of the Tao in Chinese philosophy is used when this passage is translated into Chinese, so that Mandarin and Cantonese speakers both say, "In the beginning was the Tao, and the Tao was with God and the Tao was God." The Tao is a neuter term, so we can see how, as ideas are translated, the genders are often flip-flopped.

This idea of the "Word" or "Wisdom" of God was very important to the early Christians. In the Christological disputes of the 2nd and 3rd centuries, both the orthodox and heretical camps used the argument that Holy Wisdom was the pre-incarnate Christ to prove their points.

Thus, for Christians the story of the Christ does not begin with Jesus, but with the beginning of the world, with Sophia-Christ, as some theologians call her, through whom all things were made, and who is, as Paul says in today's reading, "the first-born of all Creation."

Now do you see why I got in trouble at the nursing home?

Here is another term which deserves unpacking: the concept of the first-born. In ancient cultures, it was the first-born son who inherited the father's wealth and social status. Though we are usually more egalitarian today, this was an important concept for the Jews. In flipping to the masculine "Word," John is able to describe Christ as the "first-born" son of all Creation. Here he is speaking about Christ's status. All the power and glory possessed by God the Father belongs by extension to him as well, since Sophia-Christ was the first being created.

This flies in the face of that later orthodox formulation stating that Christ is "co-eternal with the Father," without beginning or end. This is a fine theology, of course, but it isn't scriptural. It is also not something that needs to be explained away. The history of the church is filled with many such interesting contradictions that only serve to make our tradition richer and more multi-valent.

Another holdover from ages past is the attribution of Christ as "Lord." This really makes little sense to us Americans, as we have lived in a non-monarchical democracy for over two centuries. We no longer have "lords" and "ladies" and so for us the term has simply come to be a synonym for God, but freely floating and without meaning. The practice comes from the ancient Hebrews, who substituted the word "Adonai" whenever the word "Yaweh" appeared in the text, as it was considered blasphemy to actually utter God's name. Thus "Adonai," or "the Lord," was substituted even in translations. Whenever you see LORD in all capital letters in your own Bible, it is actually the word "YHWH" or "Yahweh" in the Hebrew.

Since God was seen as the "King of Kings," or simply the monarch amplified to cosmic proportions, "Lord" was an appropriate substitution. But is it appropriate for us? As it is a word largely without meaning for us, I would argue against it. But a greater argument against such usage is theological: Jesus said himself that "I do not call you servants, but friends." The meaning of the incarnation is that such petty and human attributions of glory and class are meaningless to God, who desires to be our friend, not our master. Process Theology confirms this by proposing that God does not have the power to coerce, only to persuade—a trait exemplified by Jesus.

And it is this very point of humility, of vulnerability, of turning the world's expectation on its ear that is illustrated so movingly in the story of Jesus' birth.

As we have seen, the early Christians believed that the Christ of God was always with God and shared God's glory. In Process Thought, we would call Wisdom or the Word the Creativity of God, the infinite potentiality that informs and inspires the Creation, from rocks to human beings. Now this makes sense: if God's "mind" is God's transcendent, Primordial Nature, then God's Wisdom or God's ideas reside there.

But the story really catches us when this Christ springs forth from the earth, not as a King in a palace, not as a triumphant warrior, as in some mythologies of the Messiah, but as a mewling pauper infant in a borrowed stable. The cognitive dissonance this creates is exactly what lends the story its charge: the trappings of prestige and power mean nothing to God. And further-more, Jesus preaches, God detests them.

For the Messiah to be born in such a place was scan-dalous. *Skandalon* in Greek means "stumbling block," and Jesus' birth certainly was that. Whether Jesus was really born "of a virgin" is a point of great debate amongst theologians, and there are many theories. The most popular of course is the affirmation of the tradi-tional miraculous birth. Most contemporary theolo-gians, however, see the virgin birth in a more mythic or metaphorical light.

My personal suspicion is that Jesus was, in fact, an illegitimate child. For the Messiah to have been born of such low estate was probably too much for the early church to swallow, and the "birth in a stable" motif sub-stituted instead. It was still scandalous, but not *so* scan-dalous as to taint Jesus' reputation as a man of God.

Another interpretation is that Mary's virginity is a Gnostic overlay. The Gnostics were a group of quasi-Christian sects that the early Church fought hard to keep from corrupting orthodox teaching. They were not always successful, unfortunately. The Gnostics did not believe that Jesus could possibly have taken a real human body, since flesh is inherently evil, and such a high spiritual being as the Christ could not possibly be in union with it. Some Gnostics even taught that while Jesus could urinate, he could not defecate: such would simply be too scandalous.

The orthodox believers had to fight for Jesus' humanity. For the most part they succeeded: Jesus was proclaimed to be both fully human and fully divine. Mary did not fare so well, for the idea that Jesus could actually have emerged from something so corrupt as human intercourse was simply too scandalous for the Gnostics. Thus, though Jesus' humanity was rescued, a real human birth was not.

The mythic nature of divine births is well attested to in world mythology. The Buddha was even born from his mother's side, since coming through the birth canal was, again, "too scandalous" to consider. The Virgin Birth is one of those issues which every Christian must decide for him or herself.

Regardless of how Christ was born, the fact is that he lived and died a very human life. And it is the testimony of the disciples that in him they felt they had caught a glimpse of God's own warmth and concern, God's own personality. As Paul says, "He is the image of the invisible God." And it is this very important word "image" that I would like to highlight. I believe this is the entire key to understanding Jesus' life and death.

Jesus' life is an icon for what is true all the time: God is always wedded to Creation, wholly and completely, present to it and having compassion for it. Jesus is a symbol, a face in which we can see the love of the Creator, a God who is concerned about people and animals and the world, who has the vision of a community where peace reigns over all.

In formulating a Christology, most theologians fall into one of two camps: those who advocate a "high" Christology and those who advocate a "low" one. A high Christology says that God "came down" to earth to be born as Jesus of Nazareth. This is the traditional, "orthodox" view. A low Christology teaches that Jesus was a charismatic teacher who had a genuine and intimate relationship with God, and through whom God spoke in an extraordinary way. Both are capable of affirming Christ's divinity, although a low Christology generally does this by affirming divinity in all of Creation as well.

Both options are available for Process thinkers; I will describe a couple of examples. In Process Thought, we call the "will of God" God's "Initial Aim." God has intentions for the universe, but because creatures are at all times free to embrace or reject God's "aim," God is always ready with contingency plans, some of which pan out and some of which don't. God is intimately concerned with the evolution of the world and provides all creatures with this "Initial Aim." We hear it in our dreams, in our conscience, in our art. Sometimes we listen. Sometimes we don't.

A high Process Christology would say that Jesus took God's Initial Aim for his own, affirming that Jesus still had a personal, Subjective Aim, but that it was either on the back burner or it was so congruent with the Initial Aim of the Divine Parent that little distinction is discernable.

A low Process Christology would say, however, that what made Jesus special was this: God's Initial Aim was whispered, and Jesus listened and responded, making of his life a creative collaboration with the spirit of God. In such an understanding, Jesus' magic is that in him we see what it means to be truly human, to be whole.

You must decide for yourself which makes more sense to you, but I myself tend towards a low Christology. I believe that it does no disservice to Jesus to say that in him God's Initial Aim found an artist and prophet who had the same passion for justice and compassion as God; that by being most fully, most unfearfully himself, Jesus fulfilled the potential that God desires for each of us.

God threw the ball, Jesus caught it and gave it a twist of his own, tossing it back to God, forming a lifelong artistic collaboration marked by trust and a sense of relatedness to all that he encountered. Because his aims were so congruent with God's, the Word was able to manifest through him, changing human history forever.

We are not alone in trying to understand this mystery of incarnation. Not long after Jesus was gone, the Church sought to understand the relationship between this peculiar man and the principle of incarnation in all of creation. This led early Christian thinkers to associate Jesus with Sophia, whom we discussed earlier, and in the third and fourth centuries to develop the rich theology of the Cosmic Christ: the Body of Christ which encompasses all of Creation. Paul says "in him do all things live and move and have their being" (Acts 17:28). Thus Christians could affirm the goodness of Creation, "the image of the invisible God," that universalized the sacrilization of the incarnation event. In other words: now the whole universe embodies God.

You'll remember from our discussions of the bi-polar nature of God that this sounds amazingly similar to God's imminent, or "Consequent Nature," the universe as God's Body, or in Christian terms, the Body of Christ.

So if God's transcendent nature is the Father, the Creator, and God's imminent nature is the Son, the Christ, you might be asking "Where does the Holy Spirit fit into the picture?" That is a question we must leave for another chapter—hopefully a shorter one! It is enough for us here to see that, in philosophical terms, this Jesus embodied the Initial Aim of God's Primordial Nature. Or in theological terms, "the Word was made flesh, and dwelt among us."

*Holy and living God,*
*in the person of Jesus Christ you have given us*
*a sublime mystery which we are still trying to unpack.*
*How can we fathom a love*
*which stretches to the very beginnings of time?*
*How can we appropriately respond*
*to the nurture which spans every galaxy,*
*known and unknown to us?*
*We cannot, and so we come to you in our limitation,*
*in our humility, and we lay at your feet our theologies,*
*our "best guesses," our wrestlings with angels,*
*and we ask your blessing, that we may simply "be with"*
*this mystery of incarnation, that we may listen*
*to your still small voice, and that,*
*as Christ's body on earth,*
*we may enter into creative collaboration with you.*
*For we ask this in the name of the one who heard*
*and spoke your Holy Word, even this Jesus Christ. Amen.*

*Truth did not come into the world naked,*
*but through symbols and images.*
*We cannot apprehend it any other way.*
*Rebirth is attained through the symbol of rebirth.*
*One can only be reborn through an image.*

The Gospel of Philip

# Chapter Five

*He suffered under Pontius Pilate,*
*was crucified, dead, and buried.*
*He descended into hell.*
*On the third day he rose again.*
*He ascended into heaven,*
*and is seated at the*
*right hand of the Father.*
*He will come again to judge*
*the living and the dead.*

The faith of my childhood was very different than the one I claim today. Things were simpler then, more black and white, starker. There was little room for relativism; some things were just right and some things weren't.

One of the things that wasn't "okay" was anything smacking of Roman Catholicism. Catholicism was considered idolatry. We were terrified of Catholics, in fact, and of the slippery slope that acceptance of them might bring. This is not to say that we didn't have Catholics for friends, but we were adamant about God's distaste for their "idolatrous" ways: their statues, their crucifixes, their robes, their icons; all of these were counted as profane obstacles to true faith. Not surprisingly, our churches were spartan in appearance. There was colored glass, but no stained glass to speak of; we had a cross, but that was as much decoration as was allowed. Anything else would be "gaudy" and "Popish."

When I got to college, however, everything changed. I was going through a spiritual crisis, and in answer to my prayers God led me, quite miraculously, I thought, to the Episcopal Church. To put it bluntly, I was blown away by what I experienced: for in the Mass, no gesture, no vestment, no ornamentation was without meaning. Everything used in worship, every decoration pointed beyond itself to something greater, something ineffable—to God.

As a poet and an artist, I live in a world of symbols, and when I found the Episcopal Church, I realized that I had been imaginationally impoverished for my entire religious life. This church gave me symbols and signs, more than I could take in, more than I could unpack. I found my senses to be almost deluged with meaning, and even now, after nearly ten years, I still haven't fully savored every gift this tradition has given to me.

What I have gotten from it, loud and clear, is the importance of symbols to human beings. We have a profound need for images, a need to express our deepest spiritual yearnings by material, human means.

Jesus understood this. The recently discovered *Gospel of Philip* testifies that "Truth did not come into the world naked, but it came in types and images. One will not receive truth in any other way." So Jesus told us stories, and he lived his life in such a way as to reveal God's glory. We already noted in our last chapter that the incarnation, Jesus' birth, is a symbol, a reminder of what is true all the time: that God is not separate from Creation, but is in union with it.

You will probably not be surprised to discover that Jesus' birth is not the only healing symbol in Jesus' life. His ministry with the disciples was a symbol for the coming Kingdom, or Community of God, a symbol we have transferred to the Eucharist. But also very important are the symbols of Jesus' death and resurrection.

In the passion narratives we are told that Jesus was mocked, spit upon, struck, and tortured. But even in the midst of it, did Jesus ever say, "Enough of this, I'm outta here"? No. Jesus stuck it out. He stayed and took it. He did not abandon us, regardless of what we did to him.

All the way to Calvary, Jesus remained with us. And even when we had nailed him to a cross, he did not leave us alone. Even though he felt betrayed, he did not betray us. Even though we cursed him, brutalized him, spit on him and murdered him, he stayed with us until his dying breath.

And it is the same yesterday, today and always. Even though we curse him, even though we brutalize each other, even though we are poisoning the earth, God stays here with us. Even though we torture one another, even though we operate out of fear and mistrust, even though we betray our brother with a kiss, or a shady business deal, or a bag of crack cocaine, God does not abandon us.

That crucifix on your wall is an image, a symbol, a snapshot of what is true for all time. No matter what we do, no matter how we grieve God, no matter how much pain and suffering we cause to ourselves and others,

*God is with us, even unto the end of the world.* That crucifix is the covenant of God with us: I am not going to
abandon you. I am not coming down off this cross until
it's over. I am here to stay!

And God is still here, remaining in union with all
flesh; your flesh, my flesh, bearing our pain, our suffering, and our sins until the end of the world, when this
earth gives up her last gasp and says "It is finished."
God is here and God is not leaving. God is here and
God is not giving up. God is here and loves you enough
to remain on the cross of your hearts and minds and
souls no matter who you are, what you have done, or
what you may ever do. Despite our ghastly offenses,
God remains enfleshed among us.

That is the great and august meaning of the crucifixion, not that Jesus had to satiate God's bloodlust by
being the once-and-for-all human sacrifice, but that in
the crucifixion Jesus shows us what is true for all time.

Alan Watts wrote that "God has wedded himself to
humanity, has united his divine essence with our
inmost being 'for better for worse, for richer for poorer,
in sickness and in health' for all eternity....The fact is
the fact: we have been given union with God whether
we like it or not, want it or not, know it or not" (Watts,
Alan. *Behold the Spirit* [New York: Random House,
1972], pp. 74-75). And God is not going to leave us or
let go of us. Ever.

The Creed tells us that Jesus then "descended into
hell." There is a great tradition of Jesus' harrowing of
Hell. The *Gospel of Nicodemus* gives us the whole story,
and a ripping good yarn it is, too. But we mustn't mis-

take early Christian mythology for doctrine. What this clause is telling us is that, unlike what some folks were saying, Jesus wasn't just "pretending" to be dead. He really, physically died. He was so dead that he passed to the land of the dead.

This is telling us that Jesus' life was no sham. He did not just "seem" to suffer; he did not simply "appear" to die, he really died, really embraced the whole of the human experience, from messy birth to painful death. Orthodox theology states that "God cannot redeem what God does not assume." Thus, God in Jesus ran the gamut. Scripture tells us that God is everywhere, from the highest heaven to the deepest pit of Hell. Process Theology teaches no less.

And even though Hell is the antithesis of community, the great isolation from others or from oneself, even there Jesus did not go alone. Jesus in Hell is another image, an image of God's ubiquity, his immanence throughout all of time and space. This clause reveals to us that even if there are alternate universes, even if there are other realities, God is there too.

But the greatest image is the resurrection, for it is in the trinity of death, banishment, and resurrection that we see the hopeful sign of God's promise: that death will not be the final word, that all things in the universe are involved in a constant dance of death, fallowness, and new life. The earth's seasons are another image of this same truth. We also know the truth of this in the scripture of our own lives: that when we enter willingly into death, allowing ourselves to grieve, God will turn our "mourning into dancing" (Ps. 30:11). All things will be made new.

There has been a lot of talk recently about the historicity of the resurrection. Many scholars following Bultmann's lead in "de-mythologizing" the gospels deny the possibility of an actual physical resurrection. They say instead that the early Christians were amazed that even after Jesus' death, they continued to feel his presence in their midst, especially in their celebration of the Eucharist. They interpreted this continued sense of Jesus' presence in the only terms available to Jews of their time: as a resurrection.

Gnostic Christians taught that, since Jesus had only been a spirit all along, pretending to be a man, the resurrection was a spiritual one. Others, though, say with Paul, that "if Christ be not [physically] raised, our faith is in vain."

Unfortunately, the gospel writers are not clear on this point. After the resurrection, Jesus inexplicably shares properties of both spiritual and physical beings. When he first appears to the disciples, huddling in their locked upper room, he walks through the walls like a ghost. Yet when Thomas goes to put his hand into the holes in Jesus' hands, they are solid. What are we to make of this?

Evangelical theology solves the problem by saying that after the resurrection, Jesus had a "glorified" body unlike his earthly body, which is at the same time related to the physical body and yet "more than" it was. Evangelicals go on to teach that we too will have similar "glorified bodies."

Process Theology allows for a similar conclusion. Quantum physics has revealed that none of the things which we take to be solid matter actually *are* solid. In fact, we are made up of much more empty space than we are of anything solid. And when you get right down to it, even the "things" the very atoms we are supposed to be made of are themselves illusions caused by sub-atomic particles leaping in and out of existance.

We are all energy beings, and not matter after all. Matter is an illusion. This is not New-Age claptrap, this is solid scientific theory. And if we are willing to accept energy beings which can be seen by our limited sense organs, should we not be willing to accept energy beings which may exist according to different laws? "There are more things in heaven and earth, Horatio, than can be found in your philosophies," Hamlet reminds his friend—and us.

It would suprise me, then, if life were to end with the death of the physical body. Everything in us points to the hope that we somehow continue a conscious existence. I do not deign to predict what sort of exis-tence it may be, but I am saying that we cannot rule it out scientifically. Rather we must trust the more subtle evidence presented by mythology—and the heart—to tell us what is true on this issue.

Like the Virgin Birth, the resurrection of Jesus is something you must decide for yourself. It is not an insurmountable hurdle. I cannot tell you what hap-pened. What I do know is this: that myth is more important than history.

History, regardless of what happened to Jesus, is dead and buried, but myth lives on in each and every one of us. Myths are the stories that make sense of our lives. Regardless of what you think of the resurrection, the story still stares you in the face and says, "Deal with me." The historicity of the Resurrection might be debatable, but the truth of the cycle of death and rebirth is not. For here, God has given us another symbol, another image with which to behold that which is true for all time.

The Ascension is another oft-disputed scene. Luke tells us that Jesus spent several weeks with the disciples after his resurrection, and then rose out of sight from the top of a mountain. This is certainly poetic imagery, as we no longer believe that God is "up there in the sky." We now know that up in the sky is only outer space, but the disciples did not know that. If, on top of a mountain, Jesus in his ghostly resurrection body finally passed "beyond" it might very well appear to them that he vanished into heaven. What is more important to me, though, is the implications of such an action.

By going "beyond" Jesus was no longer limited to a physical body which could only be in one place at one time. One Eucharistic prayer issued by the Episcopal Church says that Christ "ascended into heaven to fill all things." That is an image worth clinging to. That this same personality, this Jesus who showed us God's face, who revealed to us the kind-hearted personality of the Creator, now fills every corner of the universe. It describes the early Christians' experience; that wherever they went, the spirit of Christ was present and available to them in an obvious and powerful way.

The final clause which we will consider in this chapter has to do with judgment, with the return of Christ as Judge. Most Christians today are not eager to go around making end-of-the-world predictions based on the book of *Revelation* or other apocalyptic sources. Jesus promised that "no one would know the day or the hour." Instead, we are to be faithful and to work hard until the time arrives.

Evangelical Christians, however, have worked out an elaborate end-times scenario which begins with a rapture, continues through seven years of suffering, and ends with the battle of Armageddon. But this is not the historical view of the church. Most mainline Christians today see the second coming of Christ as an ideological rather than a physical arrival. As Christians we are moved by God's Spirit and by the life that we share in community to bring the Good News of justice and liberation and peace to the nations, and we are entreated to work towards that day when all peoples shall know what it is to be free, when poverty is a dimly receding memory, and when God will wipe the tears from our faces.

The second coming will arrive when we fulfill our promise to be Christ's body on earth, creating the Community of God, the seed of which Jesus planted here in the church. But, you might say, it's been two thousand years and we still haven't got it right. But I would remind you that two thousand years is the blinking of an eye as far as this seventeen-billion-year-old universe is concerned. The human race has had a lot of growing up to do. Call me an optimist, but I think we're doing fine.

I do not care to speculate about God's judgment— that is in God's hands. It is a mystery to us, and should be. But there is also a way in which Christ is judge in the here and now.

We have not been the church Jesus has called us to be. It is the constant comparing of what we the church are doing to Jesus' teachings that is Jesus' judgment of us. By Jesus' words we judge that our ancestors didn't do so well. By Jesus' words we judge that we are not doing much better. At every turn we should be asking ourselves, "Are we being Jesus to each other?" By this means we allow Christ to judge and direct our decisions, our motivations, and our future.

And we need not look only to the past. In our daily, intimate relationship with God, the Holy Spirit can be trusted to whisper to us God's truth—in our dreams, in our relationships, through the church, and yes, through the many many symbols that God has given us as our rich inheritance.

> *Jesus, you spoke to the disciples in stories,*
> *you spoke to countless generations of your followers*
> *through the images and symbols of the liturgy,*
> *in artwork, and in the "visual sermons"*
> *of stained glass and mystery plays,*
> *but it is in the symbols of your life,*
> *of your death, and of your triumphant resurrection*
> *that we are struck to our core,*
> *where the sublime mysteries of your love*
> *and depth of concern are revealed.*
> *Help us to see you where we do not expect to.*
> *Help us to trust in your guidance and grace;*
> *and give us hope and a heart to work*
> *for the coming of your Community,*
> *where all beings will cry with one voice*
> *in praise of your redemption. Amen.*

*The Spirit helps us in our weakness;*
*for we do not know how to pray as we ought,*
*but that very Spirit intercedes*
*with sighs too deep for words.*
*And God, who searches the heart,*
*knows what is the mind of the Spirit,*
*because the Spirit intercedes for the saints*
*according to the will of God.*

Paul's Epistle to the Romans

# Chapter Six

## I believe in the Holy Spirit

When I was a boy—I must have been all of five years old—I remember thinking that I would feel much more comforted if God were sleeping next to me in bed. So I would scoot over to make sure God had room, and I would try to go to sleep balanced recklessly on the edge. It's a good thing I didn't have much of a notion of the trinity at the time, because there wouldn't have been room for *me* in my bed! I would have had to leave the bed to God, all three of "him," and go and sleep on the couch, which would have missed the entire point of wanting to fall asleep snuggled up next to God.

I did learn about the trinity eventually, and came to embrace the concept. And chances are that if you are a Christian, unless you are a Unitarian or a Jesus-only Pentecostal, you are also a Trinitarian. Trinitarians believe that God is possessed of three co-equal, co-eternal and consubstantial, yet distinct personalities: the Father, the creator of all that is; the Son, who encompasses in his body all that is; and the Holy Spirit, the nurturer and supporter of all that is.

The doctrine of the Trinity is not a biblical doctrine at all, but an invention of the early church. The early Christians noted that they encountered God in three ways: through their Jewish tradition, which spoke of a loving Creator, through their experience with Jesus, and after the resurrection, with a comforting presence burning in their breasts.

You may be asking, "Why just three? Might we not encounter God in other ways, through other personalities?" You would be right in asking this, and you would also most likely be right. When we look at the religions of the world, God appears to the people of the Earth in myriad forms and faces, any one of them capable of mediating salvation and grace.

Yet there is still something magical about the number three. Hindus have a trinity consisting of Brahma, the creator, Shiva, the destroyer, and Vishnu, the sustainer. In Celtic mythology, too, we find the triple goddess: the Maiden, the Mother, and the Crone. Early Christian experience embraces this "three-ness" and gives it to us as our working model.

Why is "three-ness" important to us? Hasn't it caused us all kinds of problems since our very beginning, to be accused of polytheism? Sure it has, but it has also brought with it an indispensable revelation: that of *God as community*. When Jesus declares to the disciples that "the Community of God is amongst you," he is testifying to this reality: that God is not found in isolation. That, we call Hell. No, God is only found "in the midst of us," in the life of community. The doctrine of the Trinity reveals to us that even God must be a community—the living and striving, in tandem, of three persons (as the Eastern Church would say) or three personalities (as the Western Church would say).

We have already discussed at length two of the three persons or personalities involved—the Creator and the Christ. But what of this elusive third? When we think of the Creator, oftentimes we think of a grand old man or, more recently, even an old woman or crone. When we think of Christ, we see the face of Jesus or we remember Wisdom calling in the marketplace. But what of the third, the Holy Spirit? What kind of face does this one wear?

We aren't used to thinking of the Holy Spirit as much of a person in our tradition. We give lip service to the notion, but no image, no face springs to mind. The Holy Spirit is more of a phantom, an "idea" that we live with rather than a person. I think the Holy Spirit has gotten a short shrift for a long time. Let's take a look at "her" long history in our tradition, and try to figure out how we connect with "her" today.

I say "she" since the Hebrew word for spirit—*ruach*, or "wind"—is feminine, as is the Greek *pneuma*. In early Jewish mythology, God would be the source of both Holy Spirits *and* evil spirits; Holy Spirits such as the one who filled Joshua at the passing of Moses, and evil spirits, such as those that came upon King Saul and gave him his madness.

There was not a distinction as to their source at that time: God was the source of all things, both good and evil. The concept of a devil as God's shadow side had not yet developed, so all supernatural entities found their source in God. We find this moral ambivalence on God's part all throughout the Old Testament. It wasn't until the Babylonian exile that the Jews began to stratify and quantify the celestial hierarchies.

During all this time that the Old Testament was being experienced and written, however, God's Spirit does begin to take on her own personality. It is the Spirit who gives Samson his extraordinary strength (Jud 14:6), and who inspires the artistic skill of Besaleel (Ex 36:1ff). These are "inspirations," literally, "the spirit inside," prompting the creativity and resolve of these men.

In the prophetic material, however, we hear the Spirit speaking God's own voice. Isaiah tells us, "The spirit of GOD is upon me, because the HOLY ONE has anointed me. God has sent me to bring good news to the oppressed, to bind up the brokenhearted, to proclaim liberty to the captives, and release to the prisoners; to proclaim the year of the HOLY ONE'S favor, and the day of vengeance of our God; to comfort all who mourn" (Is. 61:1-2).

It is this Spirit who came upon the various prophets, sometimes in startling ways, and gave them utterance of God's words—often words the political authorities did not want to hear. Thus, the Spirit is also sometimes associated with madness, since no one in their right mind would endanger their own life just to get God's message across. "Of course the Spirit has come upon Elijah, for Elijah is a sane man, and would never say such things himself!"

Later, as literacy became important to the Jews, the Spirit became the bestower of intellectual faculties, as the writer of Sirach informs us when he writes, "If the Holy One is willing, one will be filled with the spirit of understanding."

Thus, the Holy Spirit, although not worshipped *as* God by the Hebrews, certainly testifies *to* God and speaks *for* God in the Old Testament. These themes are developed further when we reach the New Testament, as you might expect. Here, the Spirit is portrayed as much more extrovert, as more of a major player in the story from the very beginning, for it is in Matthew's Gospel that we see the Holy Spirit coming upon the maiden Mary, and begetting in her a child, the Word.

This image is very important: the Spirit as the Begetter of the Word. It is important because, like so many images from the life of Jesus, it is a portrait of something which is true for all time, as we will elaborate below.

The Holy Spirit plays a supporting role in Jesus' ministry. It is the Spirit which descends as a dove from heaven to declare God's anointing upon Jesus at his baptism. It is also the same Spirit who supports him in the wilderness during his temptation by Satan (Mk 1:12).

But according to Jesus, the primary role of the Spirit is to *take his place* once Jesus is gone. Jesus promised in John's Gospel that after he has gone back to the Father, he would send the Spirit, who would "teach you everything, and remind you of all that I have said to you" (Jn 14:26).

After Jesus' resurrection, the *Gospel of John* shows Jesus breathing the Holy Spirit into the disciples, much

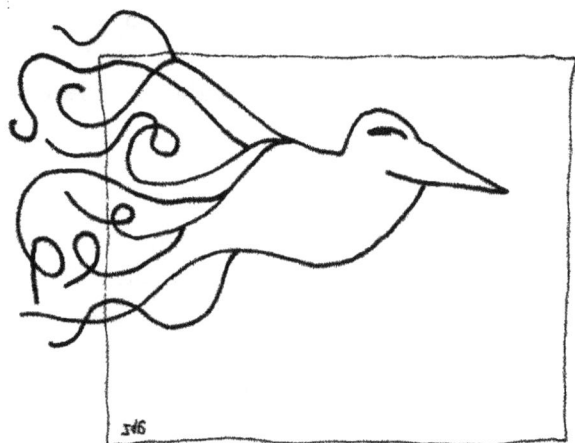

like God breathed life into Adam; Jesus breathes on them and says, "Receive the Holy Spirit."

The most dramatic of the Holy Spirit's appearances, however, is at the Feast of Pentecost. Luke tells us, "When the day of Pentecost had come, they were all together in one place. And suddenly from heaven there came a sound like the rush of a violent wind, and it filled the entire house where they were sitting. Divided tongues, as of fire, appeared among them, and a tongue rested on each of them. All of them were filled with the Holy Spirit and began to speak in other languages, as the Spirit gave them ability" (Acts 2:1-4). This seems to be the Spirit's extrovert peak in scripture, and modern Pentecostals testify that God the Spirit is just as noisy nowadays as "she" was back then.

Except for the modern Pentecostals, the history of the Holy Spirit has been spotty ever since. For many of the Patristic writers, especially Origen, the church itself is the primary sphere of the Spirit's influence on the world. Many heretical disputations were argued and settled over the validity of the Spirit's Godhood, but no controversy has been so upsetting and unsettling as the Filioque clause in the Nicene Creed.

We use the Apostles' Creed in our parish, but we cannot speak about the history of the Spirit in the church without mentioning this other very important Creed. Ratified in 325, at the Council of Nicea, the Nicene Creed contained the phrase, "I believe in the Holy Spirit, who proceeds from the Father." This is the original wording and is still retained in the East. The Eastern church, though counting all three persons of the trinity as equally God, also affirms that some persons in God are more equal than others, namely, God the Father. Eastern theology puts God the Father on the top of the triangle, with the Son and Spirit subordinate beneath him.

Then, in the eleventh century, the Pope at Rome decreed that a long-debated insertion be added to the Creed. This states, "I believe in the Holy Spirit, who proceeds from the Father *and the Son.*" This is still how we recite the Nicene Creed in the West, and it has caused no end of difficulty in East-West church relations, as you might expect. This turns the divine triangle on its ear, and makes the Spirit subordinate to both the Father *and* the Son.

Did the Pope of Rome have the *authority* to change a document ratified by the whole church in the fourth century? The Eastern Church says "No!" and any honest historian must agree. Still, we are stuck with it. Good or bad, it is our heritage as Western Christians.

You might be saying to yourself, "What difference does it make? Isn't this all speculation anyway? Isn't the Spirit going to do "her" job regardless of how we try to explain it?" You are quite right. I do not believe God gets overly concerned with our petty theological squabbles, except when such squabbles get in the way of *important* work, which they frequently do. So I suggest that at this point we dispense with history and talk about the work of the Holy Spirit in the present.

As we have evaluated our faith in the light of Process thought, we have painted a picture of God the Creator as God's transcendent, Primordial Nature: eternal, constant, the source of infinite potentiality, and of God's intended direction for the universe's evolutionary unfolding.

And we have portrayed the Christ as God's immanent, or "Consequent Nature." This is the "Cosmic Christ" whose personality we meet in Jesus and whose body encompasses the whole of the created order: every galaxy, every sun, every star and flower finds its home in Christ, in whom St. Paul says all things "live and move and have their being."

These two "parts" of God are usually the only two needed in Process Theology. Pure Whiteheadian theology advocates a binity rather than a Trinity. But as you might expect, many Christian Process theologians are not happy with that. Nor am I happy with most of the answers proposed by the newer Process theologians. They all seem to become so abstract as to be conceptually and practically useless. And, as Occam's Razor states, "the simplest explanation (that takes into account all the facts) is probably the right one."

So where does the Holy Spirit fit in? It fits in *in us*. Jesus said that he would send "a comforter" who will give us the words and wisdom we need. It is my opinion that the Holy Spirit is the spark of God that is conscious in us, the voice that whispers to us. It is the conscience that pricks us, it is the source of our dreams, good and bad, it is the Holy Spirit that inspires us to courageous acts and divine works of art. The Holy Spirit is the interface between God's transcendent nature and God's immanent nature.

The Eastern Christians are right when they say that the Holy Spirit proceeds from the Father, for it is the warming, hallowing presence of the Spirit of God in us that speaks to us the creativity and the Wisdom of God's transcendence. But the Spirit is also the doorway through which we speak back to God. Or, as the thirteenth century Christian mystic Meister Eckhart said, "The eye with which I see God is the same eye with which God sees me."

In this way the West is correct that the Holy Spirit also proceeds from the Son, the created universe, back to the Father. It is our own experience, our own growing, our own changing that is communicated by the Spirit back to God's Primordial Nature, the Father. And through this communication God the Father gains experience, grows and changes and evolves *with* the universe through time.

The Holy Spirit is that spark of God that is in us: that candle to which we talk when we pray, that fire in our breast when we have been blessed. Christ is the God of which we are a member, God's body, the cosmos; but the Holy Spirit is God who is a part of us, our body, our imaginations, the source of our dreams and the hearer of our prayers.

And so, although we ourselves are the Body of Christ, it is through the Spirit that we hear God's voice, God's ideas, God's Initial Aim for the universe and for our own lives. It is this still, small voice that gives utterance to our deepest groanings in prayer, that gives us the words to speak in stressful situations, that inspires us to new heights of creativity, that gives us the courage and comfort to do and say dangerous things in the cause of liberty and justice.

I said earlier that the image of the Holy Spirit begetting the Word is an important one, for it is an image which is as true for us now as it was for Jesus two thousand years ago. The Word is begotten by the Holy Spirit. God's ideas are begotten in us by the same Holy Spirit, and when we act on them, God *is made* flesh, and Christ is born again in our very midst. It is by the ministry of the Holy Spirit that we recognize ourselves as the Body of Christ; it is by the ministry of the Holy Spirit that we recognize each other as members of that same Body, and it is by the ministry of the Holy Spirit that we recognize the world as sacred.

The Holy Spirit, the one who has no face in our imaginations, is, in fact, that part of God which is most intimate with us. Perhaps this is why "she" has no face. We associate a face with "the other," and the Holy Spirit is not "other." It is God, in us, our comforter, and our sustainer. Had I known this as a child, I would have slept much more soundly, for I would have realized that God did not need for me to make room in my bed. For God already had a comfy resting place in my heart. Indeed, in the hearts of all who take notice.

> *Holy Spirit, our comforter,*
> *you are ever with us, in our waking,*
> *in our sleeping, and in our restless nights.*
> *Help us to be conscious*
> *of our relationship with you,*
> *and that our words to the Creator*
> *are ever borne by your wings.*
> *Burn brightly in us,*
> *so that we may take your fire to a world*
> *cold in its forgetfulness,*
> *comfortless in its rejection of you.*
> *Holy Spirit, come upon us with power and wisdom,*
> *to make your Good News known in all the world,*
> *for we ask this through Jesus Christ,*
> *whose very members we are. Amen.*

*The body is a unit, though it is made up of many parts; and though all its parts are many, they form one body. So it is with Christ. For we were all baptized by one Spirit into one body—whether Jews or Greeks, slave or free—and we were all given the one Spirit to drink. Now the body is not made up of one part but of many. If the foot should say, "Because I am not a hand, I do not belong to the body," it would not for that reason cease to be part of the body.... But in fact God has arranged the parts in the body, every one of them, just as he wanted them to be. If they were all one part, where would the body be? As it is, there are many parts, but one body.*

Paul's First Epistle to the Corinthians

# Chapter Seven

*I Believe in...the holy catholic Church,*
*the Communion of Saints*

C hristmas is always a magical time for a child. One of the things that added to the mystical quality of my own childhood Christmases was the ubiquitous presence of the Salvation Army outside the local K-Mart. Unlike adults, who usually find their incessant bell-ringing annoying, I was fascinated with them. It was apparent to me, even at the theologically ripe age of six, that these people were reminding shoppers that Christmas was really about Jesus. Furthermore, I decided that this was a worthy goal for my own life, and I proudly announced to my mother that when I grew up I was going to join the Salvation Army.

"What?" She drew back, with a look of shock. "You're not going to be a Baptist?"

I was stunned. I had no clue that the Salvation Army was a separate denomination. I suppose I just figured they were some kind of parachurch organization that lots of Christians joined in order to remind shoppers of the meaning of Christmas. I felt ashamed, but I learned my first big lesson in the story of the many divisions and schisms in the Body of Christ.

Most of these divisions are all pretty recent. In the first few years after that scary Pentecost display in the upper room, there was only one church, the church at Jerusalem. Other Christian groups, even though they were extremely diverse, measured their orthodoxy on whether or not they were in "communion" with this original, and very Jewish, congregation under the leadership of Jesus' brother, James. Anyone else who claimed to have a "church" was considered a heretic.

But after the destruction of the temple in the year 70 of the common era, there was no "one" church to which smaller churches could point as the source of their authority. They would have to find a new definition.

They, like us today, had to ask the question, "What is the church?" and odd as it may seem, it is not an easy question to answer. The word is attributed to Jesus only twice in the canonical gospels, and most biblical scholars agree that both instances are later additions to the text by well-meaning Christian editors.

The Greek word for church is *ekklesia*, which simply means "congregation." This is fitting, since early churches associated with the Church at Jerusalem were, like the synagogues at which they continued to worship, congregational in their associations and government. After the destruction of the temple, however, Christianity lost the plumb line of orthodoxy set by James and the apostles, most of whom had been martyred by this time. The church may have continued as a group of diverse and congregational communities had it not been for the extreme threat of the Gnostics who were infiltrating many communities and teaching dangerous, world-hating doctrines which bore no resemblance to the teachings of Jesus.

In order to counter the threat, the church chose teachers who had been taught directly by the apostles and named them bishops. In this way the churches hoped to safeguard Jesus' original teachings. If I can point to my bishop, and he can point to the bishop who taught him, and if that bishop was taught by an apostle, who was taught directly by Jesus, we can show an unbroken line of authentic, apostolic ministry, against which the Gnostics could not hope to prevail. This is the beginning of the apostolic succession. It had nothing to do with passing on "magical" priestly power, but everything to do with preserving the integrity of Jesus' teaching, a noble aim, even if the practice was to go astray later.

In the Creed, we speak of the church as "catholic," which sticks in the craw of many Protestants, even if they still recite the Creed liturgically. But what does the word "catholic" really mean? First off, it has little to do with the Church of Rome, which we call the "Catholic Church" as a kind of ecclesiological shorthand. This is misleading. The word "catholic" emerged as a result of the Gnostic threat. Here's how it happened.

Following Plato's lead, Gnostic Christians divided the world into three categories of people: hylics, psychics, and pneumatics. Pneumatics, as you might expect from the word itself, are those who are filled with the Spirit, and is the term Gnostics used to refer to

abz

themselves. They are the enlightened, who have received the "secret" teachings of Jesus. They thus possess the full measure of truth, and are free from the cycle of reincarnation.

Next come the psychics, which include you and me and all the other "orthodox" Christians. Didn't know you were "psychic" did you? "Psychic" in this case, refers to those who have head-knowledge of Jesus, but only half his teachings. According to the Gnostics, we psychics will continue to reincarnate until we receive the "full" gospel.

At the bottom of the pile are the "hylics"—those folks who haven't heard anything about Jesus, or who have not made a commitment to him, even on a "psychic" level. These folks have no hope of escaping the wheel of Samsara.

The pneumatics held their "secret teachings" close to the vest, and kept them truly secret until one's initiation. Salvation for them was for the special few, the elect, those lucky dogs who knew the "secrets." In contrast to this, the orthodox Christians began to speak of themselves as "catholic." They called themselves this because they believed that the gospel wasn't a secret to be hoarded, but Good News to be shouted from the roof tops; a message not just for the chosen few, but for all and everybody. The gospel was "universal," for everyone—which is what the word "catholic" actually means.

This battle between the historic bishops and the Gnostic heretics was a defining moment in the history of the church. It set us off on a course which was much more hierarchical, in which the original, congregational practice of the early Christians was lost completely.

The apostolic succession seemed to work fine as the means of determining Christian orthodoxy until about the year 1000, when the Bishop of Rome and the Bishop of Constantinople had a huge falling out. This precipitated the great schism, which we have spoken about before. Both bishops proclaimed the other to be heretical. They excommunicated each other, and from then on the Roman churches and the Orthodox churches have competed for the title of Christ's sole body on earth. Nobody, apparently, thought to ask Christ *his* opinion on the split, but there you have it.

Which church was the "real" church? This is a difficult question. From the second century through the time of the schism, salvation was seen as being granted only to those "inside" the church. The church was like Noah's ark: if you were on the ark, you were safe. If not, you drowned. So, after the great schism, there were two "arks"; which was the right one?

Unfortunately for Rome, any critical analysis of the events point to the Pope being in error for trying to seize power that was not historically his. And Rome paid an even higher price for its arrogance when its continued lust for power precipitated the Protestant Reformation, which led to innumerable schisms and divisions in the Body of Christ. Which "ark" is the right one now?

The other day, a pithy statement popped into my head that made me smile. The statement is this: "Theology fixes things." When we humans have a moral or spiritual dilemma, we solve our dilemma by doing theology. The medieval Roman church developed quite an elaborate map of the "church" in its own time that satisfied its own insecurities about its connection with those who had gone before.

Theologians in the middle ages spoke of the church as having three divisions: there was the "church militant," the "church expectant," and the "church triumphant."

The "church militant" was the sum total of all believers alive and living on the earth. We are the "army" of Christ, advancing his cause against the hordes of pagan barbarians. The "church expectant" referred to those trapped in Purgatory, who would one day know the bliss of the "church triumphant" or those saints enjoying the presence of God in heaven. Since Roman Catholicism has always taught that those who have gone to their reward are conscious, are aware of what is happening on earth, and are able to "root" for us and intercede for us in prayer, we speak of the sum total of these three "divisions" of the church as the "Communion of Saints." The Communion of Saints is always listening, always watching, and always ready to help with their prayers; and some of them might even have an "in" with saints, powerful angels, or even the holy mother.

Ever since the Reformation, Protestants have not been able to point to an unbroken succession of bishops as a symbol of our unity as Christ's body—so to what *can* Protestant Christians point? This Communion of Saints is a fine starting point for our understanding of the church today. For this teaches us that all believers, past, present, and future, Catholic, Orthodox, or Protestant, are all part of one transcendent body.

Protestant theology, then, holds that it is the ministry of the Holy Spirit that unites us and is now the symbol of our unity.

This is a good starting point for our discussion, however, only if our primary concern is the global church through time. But most of us do not live globally or trans-chronologically (if that is even a word). You and I are bound to this time and space. What, then, does "church" mean to us? Is it primarily the communion of Christians, world-wide? Or is it our local congregation? Or is it your circle of friends? Or is it perhaps the coming Community of God, of which the local community is but a foretaste?

For me, the church is where I encounter Christ in a dynamic way. Remember that when we look at things from a Process perspective, we cannot think of them as "things" at all, but as "events." Thus, in Process Theology, the church is present wherever the "Christ event" is happening.

Remember the gospel story of the woman who was caught in adultery? Her life was going to be over, literally, when that mob finished with her. But instead, something else *happened.* Jesus happened. Jesus stepped into the scene and changed her history forever. Jesus happens to people all the time, and our lives are transformed as a result of this encounter.

This is the church: the succession of eventful encounters with the living Christ, who transforms each and every occasion he touches. The church is an event moving through time, encountering people and transforming them until they are more than what they were. Are we a part of that? Yes, but does it happen by virtue of our just being here? Not exactly. Process Theology teaches us that we are the church precisely because of *what we do*, not because of the sign we hang outside or the kind of membership card we carry.

We are the church when we rescue a woman from unjust "justice"; we are the church when we reach out to the sick and the lonely; we are the church when we take a stand for peace; we are the church when we feed the hungry and clothe the naked; and we are also the church when we stand outside a K-Mart ringing a bell and reminding people what Christmas is all about.

> *Jesus, you prayed to God*
> *that we would "all be one"*
> *even as you are one with the Creator.*
> *But we are a diverse people*
> *and do not know how to be one people.*
> *Help us to see ourselves as your body,*
> *not by virtue of the words we speak*
> *or the color of hats we wear,*
> *but by the quality of love*
> *and concern we show others,*
> *for we ask this by virtue*
> *of your holy name. Amen.*

*The scribes and the Pharisees brought a woman who had been caught in adultery; and...said to him, "Teacher, this woman was caught in the very act of committing adultery. Now in the law Moses commanded us to stone such women. Now what do you say?" Jesus...said to them, "Let anyone among you who is without sin be the first to throw a stone at her." ...When they heard it, they went away, one by one... Jesus...said to her, "Woman, where are they? Has no one condemned you?" She said, "No one, sir." And Jesus said, "Neither do I condemn you. Go your way, and from now on do not sin again."*

The Gospel According to John

# Chapter Eight

## *I believe in...the forgiveness of sins*

I don't know about you, but I am a classic conflict-avoider. I will go out of my way to eliminate stress-ful situations. In fact, I will admit to stretching the truth when I believed it was what someone else wanted to hear, especially if that someone else was hopping mad at the time.

I remember one occasion when my wife and I had been avoiding one another. I wasn't speaking to her; she wasn't speaking to me. This went on for a couple of days, actually, and was extremely uncomfortable. And when we finally did sit down to sort it out we were both a little surprised. I told her I was avoiding her because I thought she was mad at me. She was avoiding me because she thought I was mad at *her!* So because we both assumed the other was more upset than we were, we had a miserable couple of days where we simply did not connect, where our relationship was sorely com-promised.

This diminished relationship my wife and I experienced is similar to the effect of sin upon our relationship with God. The idea that sin causes estrangement between God and the human family is one that goes back a long way in our religious history. Many cultures have myths about a "Garden of Eden," some faraway time when God and humankind were in harmony, a harmony that has somehow gone awry. In Christianity, we call this "the Fall." In Hinduism we say that the "Age of Kali" has ushered in a time of increasing disharmony. And even the ancient Chinese talk about the even more distant "Ancients" who walked in accord with the Tao.

All of these point to a human intuition that somehow, something has estranged us from God, though every culture has had a different way of dealing with the situation and restoring harmony. The word "religion" itself is from the Latin word meaning "to reconnect," and even within the same religion one might find various ways to heal the breach.

The Judeo-Christian tradition is no stranger to this dilemma and has developed several theories of how sin is to be dealt with. The Jews practiced a religion of sacrifice. They felt that transgression of God's revealed Law (handed down to us in the first five books of the Bible) forfeited the sinner's life, and that God demanded the sinner's blood, or his life, in exchange. Frequently people were put to death for their sins, which may or may not have expiated their misdeeds (the Bible is not clear on this point).

But because Yahweh is a merciful deity, he allowed for the life of an animal to take the place of the sinner.

Thus, the practice of making sin offerings was a normal part of Jewish life until the destruction of the temple in 70 C.E.

This method of atonement, or at-one-ment with God, is called "scapegoating." It gets its name from a ritual performed by the Jews on the day of atonement, when the high priest would lay his hands on the head of a goat, transferring the collective sin of Israel for the whole of the year upon this animal, who was then driven into the desert to die, carrying the sins of the people with it.

This sacrificial means of atonement has carried over into Western Christianity as well. According to St. Anselm, who defined the "Substitutionary Atonement" theory for Western Christians, Jesus was a human sacrifice offered to God with the sins of the whole world on his head. When he died, God's need for blood and justice was appeased, and the offense that kept God from enjoying intimacy with creation was removed.

While this is the theory which has almost totally dominated Western Christianity, it is far from satisfactory, and I'll tell you why: Jesus spoke a lot about forgiveness. He insisted that no retribution be taken, but that our forgiveness flow freely, "seventy times seven times," or in other words, forever.

Now it is strange that God requires of us behavior which God "himself" is unwilling or unable to model. If God demands retribution, why does God forbid it of us? And if we are capable of such forgiveness where God is not, does that not make us God's moral superiors?

Now, of course, this is ludicrous. The idea that God

demands death, of ourselves, of an animal, or especially of another human being simply because his royal dignity has been offended and "heads must roll" for God to feel okay about us is to caricature God as a bloodthirsty monster, very unlike the God of love and infinite mercy preached by Jesus.

Fortunately, Anselm's "Substitutionary Atonement" theory is not the only theory our tradition gives to us. The earliest Christians, who continued to practice their Judaism in Jerusalem under the leadership of Jesus' brother, James, believed that Jesus had come to do away with sacrifices altogether, and so did not view his death as a sacrifice. Jesus instead came to reveal the "soul" or the "spirit" of the Law which would balance the strictness of the Letter of the Law.

The West is possessed of another theory, which caused a great stir in the late middle ages, but never quite caught on to the extent that the substitutionary theory did. This other theory was put forward by the controversial theologian Abelard. Abelard taught what is called the "Moral Influence" theory, which teaches that the image of Christ on the cross is a constant reminder of the lengths that our sin can go to. We as a people were so evil, that when God came to meet us unarmed, we reacted by nailing "him" to a cross. The recognition of this should so horrify us that we turn permanently from sin and violence.

Now, although Abelard never convinced the West of his theory, I do believe he is on the right track. In the "Substitutionary" theory it is God who is estranged from humankind. The separation begins with God, and it is God who refuses communion with us until such time as his honor can be restored. In Abelard's theory, however, God is always present and willing to be in communion with us, but it is we who have hardened our hearts and turned away from God.

This is a very important distinction which needs to be explored further because I believe Abelard is correct. Process Theology teaches us that God is intimately connected, indeed enjoys mystical union, with the whole of creation, and desires nothing more than relationship, even friendship, with all creatures, including human beings. But unlike the rest of the creatures who "commune" with God naturally and un-selfconsciously, we humans are capable of "shutting off" this connection. And although we cannot escape God, we can ignore God, we can harden our hearts and refuse to hear God's voice whispering to us in the night. But *why* do we do this? Because of all the creatures of the earth, it is only humankind that are capable of deep shame.

I believe that it is because of our shame, our embarrassment, our feeling of inadequacy over what we have done, that we turn away from God; because we do not feel *worthy* of God's intimacy. As anyone who has been the recipient of real, unearned forgiveness can tell you, that kind of love is not easy to receive. Everything in us seeks to escape it. Why? Shame. It is a vicious spiral which feeds on itself, and projects its energy on those from whom we have estranged ourselves. Just like my wife and I; because we each felt that the other must be mad at us, we withdrew from intimacy with each other. Likewise, because we believe God *must* be mad at us, we have withdrawn from relationship with God; a situation God desperately wishes to correct.

This is certainly congruent with Jesus' teachings.

Jesus had no words of scorn for even the lowliest of sinners. His words and actions spoke volumes to them about the depths of God's love and forgiveness: for Jesus modeled God's own acceptance of them, just as they were. Not only that, but Jesus was able to communicate to prostitutes and tax collectors and every other sort of unsavory individual the profound truth that they were of infinite value to God, and that what they *are* is of much greater value than the things they have *done*.

In parable after parable, such as the prodigal son and the lost sheep, Jesus shows us that it is we who have gone off to a far country. God has not separated "himself" from us because of our sin. We have wandered away of our own accord, and like the youngest son who blows his inheritance on "riotous living," we are too embarrassed to return home and face our "Father." Or as Meister Eckhart in the thirteenth century put it: "God is at home—it is we who have gone out for a walk" (Fox, Matthew, OP, ed. *Meditations with Meister Eckhart* [*Santa Fe: Bear & Co., 1983*], *p. 15*)

In fact, Jesus' only words of derision were for the religious authorities who told the people that God despised them because they did not have adequate education to follow the Law properly or because they were in flagrant violation of the Law. Jesus made it clear that the only ones in flagrant violation of God's will were these very authorities who were reinforcing the people's shame and thus ensuring that they would not pursue or achieve a meaningful relationship with God; since only those who followed God as *they* did were worthy of salvation.

There are still plenty of religious authorities around

today, and the poison they spout hasn't changed much either. By keeping people focused on their own sin, they ensure that people will be so trapped by their own shame that they feel they cannot even approach God—unless, of course, they follow the strict and peculiar teachings of whatever alleged "authority" is speaking.

Jesus shows us quite clearly what we are to think of such people. Jesus said that it would be better if they were to "tie a millstone around their neck and jump into the ocean" (Lk. 17:2) than to prevent even one little one from finding a home in God's family.

I would like to point out that, so far at least, the Christian theories we have been discussing have been mostly concerned with personal sin and personal salvation. The Jews, as you will recall, have always been much more concerned with corporate or societal sin. The high priest put the sins of the whole community on the head of the scapegoat; it was the sin of the community, not just an individual, that brought catastrophe down on the heads of the people.

But for most Western Christians, the community aspect of sin and salvation has been overshadowed by an obsession with personal sin. This is largely because when the church became an institution of power, it was seen as blasphemy to criticize God's "divinely ordered" hierarchy of government in church or state. Sin, therefore, took on an increasingly personalized emphasis, with an almost morbid fascination with—and abhorrence of—sexuality and the body. Over the centuries, this myopic focus has allowed us to commit the greatest acts of human evil as a community without even flinching. Crimes we would never commit

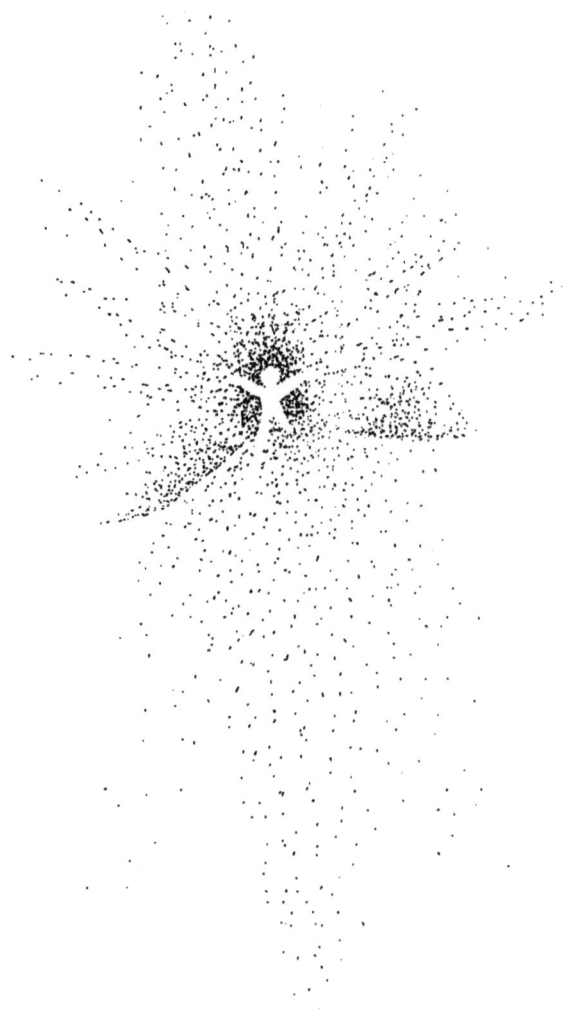

ourselves, we seem to have no problem endorsing as a people.

You or I would never kill in cold blood, yet we support governmental agencies who assassinate foreign leaders. We would never purposely starve a child, and yet we know that people are starving to death this very moment in many places in the world, and we do not as a people save them, even though we easily could. In fact, we destroy crops and other foods just to keep prices up. The more we think about it, the more we find that the gravest sins are the ones we commit together.

Christianity has not always emphasized personal sin, however. In the late second and third century, after gentile Christianity had refashioned itself along neo-Platonic lines, Christians undergoing severe persecution believed that "the wages of sin is death," as Paul tells us. The collective sin of humankind would lead to the eventual destruction or "death" of the created order. Jesus came to break death's power and to set the world free from it's entropic thrall. This, the "Christus Victor" theory of atonement, is still championed by Eastern Orthodox believers.

The Christus Victor theory envisions the earth as winding down after the Fall, falling into increasing disharmony and chaos, ruled by death and disintegration. In this theory, the crucifixion is not the event that brings salvation to humankind. Instead, it is the trick by which Jesus gains access to Hades, the realm of Death, and shatters its power from the inside out. In his resurrection Jesus triumphs over death and the grave and breaks their power forever, halting the devolution of the universe and setting in motion the eventual divinization of all things. Orthodox Christians believe that the ministry of the church on earth transfigures the entire created order to reflect the goodness and glory of God.

This is a beautiful and touching theory of atonement. We in the West can learn much from our Eastern brothers and sisters about God's mystery revealed in, through, and beyond the created order. There is a saying from the sixties that "if you're not part of the solution, you are part of the problem." Jesus himself said something similar: "Those who are not against you are for you" (Luke 9:50). In this theory, salvation is seen as being "with the program."

This is a good summary of the "Christus Victor" approach to collective salvation. Jesus has shown us that God is intimately, irrevocably united to us and to all of Creation; we participate in this salvation when we work for the transformation of society and culture to more and more closely resemble the "Community of God."

As twentieth-century Christians, we need to take a hard look at how we view atonement and our participation in it. It is important for us to see that sin is not just a personal reality, but a social one, and that the sins we do as a people need to be prophetically addressed. We need to repent; we need to change our ways. But this does not for a moment affect God's desire or ability to be an intimate partner in our daily lives. God calls each of us to come home to "relationship," to intimacy, regardless of what we have done. It is our own shame that separates us from God, not our sin. And the petty evils we are capable of as individuals are nothing compared to those we are capable of together. Yet if we individually open ourselves to God's love and forgiveness, our personal transformation cannot help but to contribute to the transfiguration of the whole. The Community of God is coming, and its seed is already planted in you.

*Compassionate and merciful God,*
*We have been staring at our navels so long*
*that we have been unable to look up*
*long enough to see you holding your arms*
*out to us, inviting us into your loving embrace.*
*Help us to forsake our guilt and shame long*
*enough to embrace you back.*
*And once we have been refreshed by your care*
*help us to model your forgiveness in our daily lives*
*until the whole earth is transfigured*
*and the Community of God is a reality in which*
*all peoples can share, for we ask this in the name*
*of thy beloved Son, through whose embrace*
*of human life we are all invited to enjoy*
*oneness with you. Amen.*

*Now if Christ is proclaimed as raised from the dead,
how can some of you say there is no resurrection
of the dead? If there is no resurrection of the dead,
then Christ has not been raised;
and if Christ has not been raised,
then our proclamation has been in vain
and your faith has been in vain.*

Paul's First Epistle to the Corinthians

# Chapter Nine

*I believe in...the resurrection of*
*the dead, and the life everlasting*

Although I do a lot of parish work, I also stay very busy ministering at two nursing homes and performing an alarming number of weddings, baptisms, and even the occasional funeral.

Now, of these latter ministries, my favorite has to be weddings. They are breezy, lighthearted affairs—when they go well—where everyone seems to be much happier than the bride and groom, who are usually stressed out and just want to get it over with. My least favorite service to do is, as you might guess, funerals.

But this is not always the case. Sometimes funerals can be very positive events, especially when the departed has lived a long, full, and happy life. Then the service is an occasion to celebrate that life, to revel in the joy that has been, and to be comforted that even greater good is to come from this goodness. I truly wish all funerals were like this. Some, of course, are not.

I recall one funeral which stands far beyond any other, as the most painful service I have ever performed. The departed was a 19-year-old skateboard punk, who deliberately shot himself in the head.

As I sat in the grandparents' backyard, I looked at the crowd that was assembling. Close to the patio the relatives were gathering: middle-aged and elderly folks who could hardly meet my gaze, so heavy was their grief. They were conservative Lutherans who had asked me to talk about Christian hope.

I pondered this. But soon I noticed that the relatives were the great minority in this quickly-filling backyard. Most of the mourners were under twenty, with shocking hair, gaudily decorated skateboards, and even more earrings than I. They met my gaze with no problem, but their stares were a challenge: their eyes said "no bullshit, preacher," and I got the message loud and clear. I also had no idea what I was going to say. How in the world was I going to satisfy both groups? How could I simultaneously give comfort both to those whose theology said that the poor boy was damned, as well as to those who had nothing but contempt for theology?

How, under such circumstances, could one talk of "hope?"

There is no denying that the goal of every one of the great religions is to offer hope, for each of them shares in the intuition that some part of the individual survives the "final portal" of death. Every religion worth its salt gives us the grace to go on with life in part simply because it affirms that our life does not end when the body ceases to function. Were it not for this promise, this intuition, many of us would fall into the slough of despair, as many nihilists or existentialists have done. Scripture tells us that "without a vision, the people perish." If we had no hope, most of us simply could not go on.

The Jews are no stranger to the intuition of individual survival beyond death. For them, life itself is linked to blood, and the concept of life without flesh and blood to experience it was completely alien to them. For the Jews, then—and for Jesus himself, as a good Jew—life after death by necessity involved a body. The resurrection of the dead was their hope. In Ezekiel we read a startling image of the valley of dry bones, upon which new flesh grows, and into which new life is breathed by God. Life after death was envisioned as embodied life, community life, not much different than life on earth as we know it, with the exception of having a divinely-ordered government, and an eternity without warfare or poverty.

The great eschatological visions of the later prophets are filled with scenes of great feasts, where all of the peoples of the earth will have their tears wiped away and will dine together at the great table of God. The lamb will lay down with the lion, and war will be heard in the land no more.

This idea of the resurrection of the dead has stayed with us. I even have relatives that refuse the notion of cremation because they don't want to make it harder for God to gather back together the ashes into their restored body. Cremation, in fact, was unheard of in the West until 1910 or so, when one of the founders of the Theosophical Society, deeply influenced by Hinduism, insisted on it. But whereas creation was the norm for Hindus, in 1910 it caused a huge ruckus in America, especially in religious circles, for exactly the same concerns as my relatives had. And though it has become commonplace nowadays, many, especially Jews and Catholics, still eschew the practice.

While the Jews were very serious about the physical resurrection of the body, the Greeks had a very different perception. The Greeks taught the immortality of the soul, positing a non-physical reality that constitutes the essence of an individual. To the soul belongs one's personality, one's memories, one's "true self"—all of which would survive after the "vehicle" of the body has dropped away. This notion was quickly adopted by Gnostics and others who saw the body and the physical world as tainted and evil, and the soul or the spirit as the pure and essential reality of a person.

St. Paul, who was deeply influenced by Greek thought, introduced these notions into the Christian vocabulary. Although Paul tried to be true to his Jewish roots by teaching that the soul longs to be embodied, it is the Greek notion of the immortality of the soul which has captured the Christian imagination throughout the ages, much more so than the Judaic resurrection, to which we have done little more than pay lip service. This has led to an increasingly individualistic view of the afterlife. A body needs community, but a disembodied spirit needs only to swim in the awesome ethereal and otherworldly presence of God.

Our tradition complements the Jewish resurrection motif with a rich and imaginative mythology of heaven, hell, and purgatory. A close examination of the biblical texts that give rise to our ideas of heaven and hell reveals them to be poetic images which are not meant to be taken literally. And yet this is exactly what our tradition has invariably done. Few thoughtful people take any part of the Revelation of John as being a literal representation of anything, and yet our most vivid depictions of the afterlife are lifted from this book as if from first-hand witnesses.

It is not surprising that we have grasped so tightly to these images, for they provide ready answers to the question that haunts every person old enough to glimpse their own mortality: "What will happen to me when I die?"

The world's religions have offered a variety of answers to this question. The Jews imagined that the dead would inhabit a shadow-world called Sheol where we await the general resurrection from the dead. The Hindus tell of countless transmigrations, where we inhabit an almost infinite succession of bodies as we mature spiritually. Perhaps the most inventive theory is offered by the Catholic church, which has concocted the non-biblical notion of Purgatory, where a soul has opportunity to be perfected until it is prepared to face the awesome reality of God's unmediated presence.

Even though this notion is unbiblical, it has much going for it. Like reincarnation, purgatory offers an individual additional opportunities to grow and mature beyond the grave. To my mind at least, this is a much more compassionate scenario than St. Paul's dictum: "It is appointed to man once to die, and after that the judgment." However, one only gets a chance to "wise up" in Purgatory if one has already embraced the gospel, however tangentially, during his or her time on earth. So even this feels like an inadequate possibility.

Perhaps the most persuasive version of Purgatory I have heard is one put forth by a twentieth-century Anglican writer named Charles Williams. A close friend and major theological influence on C.S. Lewis, Williams presents us in his many novels with a spiritual world which is very close indeed to our own. This world and the spiritual world frequently interpenetrate, giving his characters opportunity, both in this life and the next, to choose life and community, and therefore salvation, or to slink off into isolation and despair, which is Williams' notion of Hell. In Williams'—and subsequently Lewis'—vision, anyone, at any time, can choose to walk towards God or away from "him." No matter how far a sinner walks away from God, he or she can always, at any time, turn around and, like the Prodigal Son, come home. The problem is that the longer one walks in one direction the *harder it is* to turn around. Someone who has led a godly life of service is not likely to turn around and kill someone in cold blood. Likewise, a hardened sinner is not likely to put their own life on the line for a stranger.

Williams' vision has much going for it, including Patristic theology. The great neo-Platonic theologian Origen also taught that eventually, all would find their way back to the heavenly throne, including Satan himself.

But Williams' theology is more Greek than Jewish. His characters leave their bodies far behind and walk into the grey mists of the spiritual realm where moral situations may be clearer, but physical realities more obscure than ever. What are we to make of this ancient theology of resurrection? Can we simply dismiss it, as so many Western theologians have done, especially since Jesus himself arose in a glorified body, ostensibly paving the way for all of the rest of us?

My wife Kate is no fan of Paul's neo-Platonic disdain of the body. Her deepest grief is the thought of no longer being in the body that she loves so much, the body that is so often uncooperative, and yet is the sole source of so many sensations she holds sacred: the taste of good food, the ache of tiredness after a good day's work, the glorious glow after lovemaking, the sight and smell of forests, and so many other delights that simply make life worth living. And so Kate is a much bigger fan of Resurrection than of the immortality of a disembodied soul. For her the body means pleasure, people, and security.

I have to say that the skeptic in me is suspicious of the notion of resurrection, but I do sympathize with Kate's feelings. If I have learned anything about God in my short years, it is that God is a God of community and relationship, and one has to have a body for such things. In my childhood we were taught an elaborate theology concerning the "resurrection bodies" which we will someday inhabit. They will be like Jesus', glorified, incorruptible, perfect. I remember as a child imagining the resurrected Jesus as kind of like Superman: Jesus-Man, with muscles of steel, leaping the gates of Hell in a single bound, faster than a speeding sinner, rolling the stone away with one swift push. I imagined myself as having such a body some day, finally being able to beat up the bullies, able to play football worth a damn for the first time in my life.

But these thoughts seem silly to the adult "me," and are of value only for their sentimentality. But as I grew older and began to read theology, even the most sophisticated of contemporary theologians came up short. Classic Whiteheadian Process Theology provides only for something called "Objective Immortality," where the sum total of all of our thoughts and personality distinctives are reabsorbed into the transcendent nature, or mind of God, there to be available to inspire the ongoing unfolding of the universe. But this, too, is an unsatisfactory answer, as it does not take into account the widespread religious intuition of the survival of individual consciousness.

Even after all of our searching and philosophizing, we are still left with the unanswered question: "What will happen to me when I die?"

It is the one question we all want to know. Death is the biggest unknown we shall ever face. We want answers. We want unambiguous answers, something we can hang our hats on. It is probably the one question you want answered in this chapter, as well.

Very well, I am going to tell you the same thing that I told that backyard full of grieving Lutherans and skateboard punks: I don't know.

*I don't know.* I told that backyard assembly that if they wished, I could tell them about the Christian mythologies of heaven and hell, but I suspected they already knew about those. When it all comes down to it, I told them, these are only metaphors and images. We could spin our theories and theologies for hours, but if we are to have integrity, we must ultimately return to this uncomfortable place of not knowing.

I looked around at the crowd. I certainly had their attention. The Lutherans looked alarmed, but the skateboard punks looked at me with respect: perhaps for the first time they were not being condescended to; perhaps for the first time, a preacher was not bullshitting them. I took in their expectant gazes, knowing that only now could they really even hear me. I had disarmed them. Now, they wanted to be told something meaningful. Now I could talk about Christian hope.

For Christian hope has nothing to do with constructing maps of the afterlife. Christian hope does not depend on second-guessing God, or on putting our faith in pie-in-the-sky theologies that may or may not have any bearing on reality. Christian hope is very simple: God is a God of love, and God will not abandon us, in this life or the next. That's it. And it's all we need to know.

Jesus revealed to us the heart of God the Father, who loves us, provides for us, who longs to be in relationship with us, not just now, but forever. Whatever form that relationship takes is not for us to understand. In the story of Jesus' resurrection, we are given an image of eternal life that is like our own in that it involves sensation and community, but is also unlike our own in ways we cannot guess. Like the many parables Jesus told during his ministry, his resurrection is an enacted parable, pointing to both a present and a future reality. We know that resurrection is something that is happening all around us, all the time. We have all died a thousand deaths and known what it is to rise again after a time of trial. The resurrection is something we have already experienced, and know in our bones to be true.

But to what kind of reality this intuition, this knowing points, we must all stand silent.

For the truth is that when contemplating death, we are in the presence of a great mystery, exceeded only by the mystery we call God. All we can do in the presence of mystery is to be silent, to acknowledge our ignorance, and to experience our wonder. And finally, to surrender our feeble efforts to quantify it, stuff it in a box or a book, or in any other way restrain it and make it manageable. The mysteries of death and God are greater than our imaginations, greater than our ability to comprehend. God is not, after all—as C.S. Lewis says in his Narnia books—a *tame* lion. Before such mysteries we must eventually lay our best guesses down, we must finally be silent, and if we are lucky, we learn to trust.

Contemporary Judaism has said it best: "If we are faithful to God in this life, God will be faithful to us in the next."

We must learn to trust that the God who has given us birth and fed us in this life will not abandon us when we die. We must allow ourselves to be embraced by a mystery that is greater than we are, and whose love extends into realms we cannot even guess at.

What happens to us when we die? I believe that somewhere, somehow, the journey continues. And I also believe that the God who has been our constant companion will be at our side even then.

*God of mystery, companion and comforter,*
*Hold us in your warm embrace*
*as we ponder the mystery you have set before us*
*at the end of our many days.*

*Comfort us, even in our ignorance,*
*strengthen us, even in our humility,*
*and give us the grace to trust*
*that the work you are beginning in us here*
*will not be in vain, but rather only the first tottering steps*
*in an eternal life with you,*
*the joys and trials of which we cannot hope to guess at.*
*For we ask this in the name of the only one*
*who has gone beyond*
*and returned to give us hope*
*and the promise of eternal life,*
*even Jesus Christ your Son,*
*who with you and the Holy Spirit*
*reigns over every mystery*
*in heaven and earth, and yes,*
*even beyond the veil of death. Amen.*

# PART THREE

# The Sacraments

I n Part Two we focused on the Apostles' Creed, which documents those abstract notions that most Christians hold in common. In Part Three, we will turn our attention to the rites and rituals that make up the day-to-day practice of Christian worship. In other words, the Creed is what we *believe* as Christians, but the sacraments are what we *do*.

Process Theology informs both aspects. Like God's transcendent, Primordial Nature, the Creed describes those aspects of the Christian life that exist in the realm of ideas and potentialities, while God's imminent, Consequent Nature corresponds to those physical aspects that are actually acted out with our bodies. Thus, Creed and sacraments describe the bi-polar nature of Christian living that most closely corresponds to the bi-polar life of God in which we "live, move, and have our being."

The sacraments were not, as some have taught, instituted by Christ in their present form. Instead, like all aspects of all religions, they evolved as part of a process, a conversation, if you will, between the Holy Spirit and those who have faithfully—and sometimes not so faithfully—sought to discern God's Initial Aim for the cosmos. We talk, God listens. God talks, and sometimes we listen, and sometimes we don't. And so God's Initial Aim and our Subjective Aims push and pull at the trajectory of the universe in a herky-jerky movement that is, we pray, more or less heading in the direction God intends it to be going. Not perfectly, not directly, but circuitiously, slowly, excruciatingly.

But that we may someday arrive at Tielhard's Omega point, or wherever it is that God intends us to end up, this is our hope as Christians. And the sacraments are the tools that help us get there. They are seven in number: Baptism, Confirmation, Eucharist, Confes-sion, Marriage, Ordination, and Unction. Many of them are similar—there is, for instance, an awful lot of smearing with oil—but the ideas behind them are often very different. In this next section we will explore, sacrament by sacrament, what these actions, these rituals might mean for us as post-modern Christians, hopefully aided in our task by a healthy dose of Whitehead.

*Holy Baptism is the sacrament by which*
*God adopts us as his children*
*and makes us members of Christ's Body,*
*the Church, and inheritors of the*
*kingdom of God.*

The Book of Common Prayer

# Chapter Ten

## Baptism

When I was fresh out of High School, I went with my best friend Bob to a wooded piece of property owned by his family near the Oregon border for a week of camping, swimming, and overall relaxation. It was a marvelous week, and Bob and I spent a lot of it exploring a river. For several days in a row we would don sandals and bathing suits and go rock-hopping for a couple of miles downstream.

One day we discovered the most idyllic scene imaginable. It was a deep pool of dark blue water, banked by rocks as large as a house and shaded by giant trees. The wind was light, and the rustling of the leaves was counterpoint to the river's melody. Both of us were awestruck, speechless. We stood motionless for what seemed like an eternity. Finally, Bob spoke, "This is where I will be baptized." I looked at him like he was from Mars.

"What?" I asked incredulously."

"I want to be baptized," he answered, "here."

He breathed a deep sigh and closed his eyes. After a moment he opened them again and turned to me, "Will you do it? Will you baptize me?"

I hemmed and hawed for a moment. I was still a pretty strict evangelical Christian at the time, and Bob was a universalist raised by hippie parents. "Um, well," I started, flustered, "Do you even know what that *means*?"

"I know what it means to *me*," Bob said. "Will you do it?"

Well, who was I to deny him? "Sure," I said. We both gritted our teeth and entered the frigid water. Assuming the proper Baptist position for baptism, I placed my right hand on Bob's back, and kept the left one free to pinch his nose at the proper time.

"Have you, Bob West, accepted Jesus Christ as your Lord and Savior?"

"I have," he said.

I was *sure* we were going to be struck by lightning, because I knew for a fact that what Bob meant by that was not what I meant by it. Still, the proper answer had been given, and so with a shaky voice I continued.

"Then by this act you symbolize the dying of your old self and the resurrection of your new self in Christ." I pinched his nose with my left hand and leaned him back on my right until he was underwater. He broke the surface to the music of birds in the trees and sunlight flashing out from behind the thunderheads.

"Thanks," he said smiling. And I gave him a hug in congratulations, though privately, I wasn't at all sure what I was congratulating him on at the time.

Well, time goes by, and people change. I feel like I understand Bob's baptism much better now than I did then, perhaps better than he himself understood it at the time. There certainly has been little consensus on just what the act means throughout history, but we have continued to perform it just the same. Let's take a look at what it has meant to folks in various times and places—up through and including a possible Process interpretation—and perhaps Bob's baptism will make sense to you, too.

Baptism is not a ritual of Christian origin. In Jesus' own time, baptism was a familiar symbol, used in many religions, including Judaism. In fact, if you were to go up the street today to the Jewish synagogue and ask to convert, you would be baptized just as surely as you would have if you were converting two thousand years ago.

To the Jews today, baptism is a ritual of cleansing, of washing away impurities and standing before God as a whole person. It isn't so much tied to the idea of sin as it is to the idea of pure intention, of readiness, of worthiness to stand before God. Baptism signifies the voluntary "submersion" of a man or woman into the Torah, which bathes one's life with blessing.

But in Jesus' day, the baptism of John was a highly-charged political act. You see, the temple in Jerusalem was run by the Sadducees, who were largely made up of the priestly tribe. They administered the sacrifices and other rites at the temple, and although people revered the temple itself, the Sadducees were woefully out of step with public sentiment. The Sadduccees had something to lose: the temple—and with it, their jobs—if they did not cooperate, or as some would say, collaborate, with Rome. The Sadducees were also extremely secular, in spite of their position at the temple. Unlike the Pharisees and most of the populace, they did not believe in the resurrection of the dead. Furthermore, they felt that all that was needed to please God was to keep the proper ritual schedule, regardless of what was in a person's heart.

John the Baptist was a member of this tribe. His father, in fact, had been the High Priest. But instead of joining the priesthood at the temple, he rejected the whole lot of them, went out into the desert, and began to preach.

So when people started pouring out of Jerusalem in droves to hear this guy, the temple authorities were incensed. Here was this religious renegade performing sacred rites on his own authority, not under the "proper" auspices of the temple clergy at all. This was John's intention, I believe. The temple baptism had become an empty rite, like circumcision. But John preached a circumcision of the heart, not of the body.

John's baptism called people not to ritual purity, but to real, existential repentance—to turn from their ways, be totally cleansed of the past, and of their collaboration with the Roman invaders. The political connotations added another layer of meaning to the rite of baptism, making it a wild and dangerous act of political defiance, and therefore an act that carried great conviction and commitment.

And it was to John's baptism that Jesus submitted. But did it have an even different meaning for him?

I believe that it did. In all acts of baptism, something

is left behind, and something new and better is chosen. John's baptism rejected the hypocrisy of the Sadducees and the temple and instead chose nakedness before God.

But as you'll recall from Jesus' teaching, Jesus' main opponents were not the Sadducees, but the Pharisees. We can see Pharisees and Sadducees kind of like Catholics and Protestants. Sadducees were convinced that as long as the proper rituals were performed, a person was all right before God, just like Catholics might have taught before Vatican II. But the Pharisees rejected this teaching, and believed that following God's laws was what assured one's salvation. Like evangelical Protestants today, Pharisees were very strict in their behavior and very picky about their theology.

The Pharisaical tradition was the one Jesus was raised in. He was himself a Pharisee, of course, as all rabbis are from the Pharisaical school. We know now that several of Jesus' sayings in the New Testament were not original to him, but were quotes from previous rabbis, such as Hillel. But Jesus, by submitting to the baptism of John, was making a statement of his own. His baptism was a ritual turning away from legalism as the path to salvation, and the embracing of a new kind of relationship with God: one based on intention. His relationship with God was based not on rituals, not on laws, not on any outward observance, but upon the private, internal embracing of the living God as one's parent and friend.

Something died that day at the Jordan river, and something was born. So it is with all baptisms. As the Christian church began to spread, baptism became the symbol for leaving one's old religion behind and embracing Christianity instead.

But then, in the fifth century, Augustine developed the notion of original sin, and baptism in the West would never be the same. For while the Eastern Orthodox churches even today believe that everyone is born without guilt, the West followed Augustine into a terrible perversion of theology that says that we are all born bearing the guilt of Adam. This focus on sin, and especially *original* sin has been a plague on the West. It has convinced fifty generations that they were just plain born bad.

This theology caused quite a dilemma for Steven and Meg when they contacted me and asked if I would baptize their baby. We met for dinner, and Meg told me about her strict Catholic family, and how they had to have their baby baptized to satisfy her parents. But she just couldn't stand the thought that her baby was born guilty. Nor could she stand the thought that her baby had to undergo some ritual to remove some stain she didn't even believe in.

I could certainly sympathize. We had a wonderful talk about baptism for adults and baptism for children. We all agreed that when adults are baptized, it can have many meanings, of leaving the past behind, of choosing a new life. But for a child...well, that was something altogether different. I told them that the church also teaches that baptism was a ceremony of welcoming the child into the community of saints. This seemed much better to them. In the end, we worked together to construct a "welcome to earth" ceremony for their baby, Audrey. We held the ceremony in the woods, and although Meg's relatives found it very odd indeed, the fact that it was a Catholic priest performing the rites kept them from complaining too loudly. It was a lovely ceremony, and Audrey was properly welcomed.

Each of us is different inside, and each of us comes to our experiences from vastly different perspectives. Of course baptism is going to mean something unique for each one of us! For John, it was leaving the temple behind and embracing purity of heart. For Jesus, it was leaving the Pharisees and all their laws behind and embracing the God within. For Steven and Meg, it was leaving an outdated theology behind and embracing their daughter as a precious gift from God. And for Bob—for Bob I believe it was leaving the baggage of Christianity behind and embracing the Jesus of his understanding and experience.

This is congruent with Whitehead's Process Thought. Whitehead teaches that God has an Initial Aim for the universe, a direction the Spirit is trying to move the universe toward, which is always, always toward greater freedom, feeling, creativity, and novelty. The Temple cult, in John's eyes, was devoid of novelty or feeling. It was not interested in novelty or feeling. The priests' Subjective Aim moved in the direction of conformity and rote repetition. In Whitehead's system, this is the very definition of sin. When John rejected the Subjective Aim of the Temple cult, he aligned himself once again with the Initial Aim of the Spirit of the Evolving God. His baptism was a call to *metanoia*, a change of heart, of direction, of *aim*.

Likewise, the baptism of Jesus is a rejection of the strict, binding Subjective Aim of the Pharisees, as well

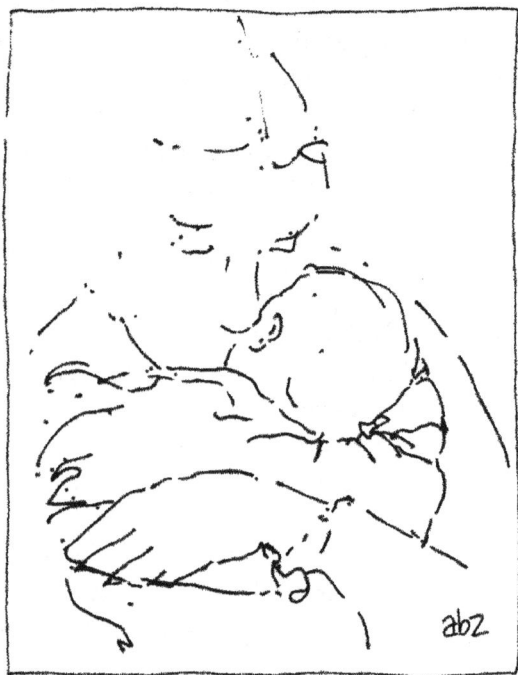

as a conscious embrace of the radical freedom of God's Initial Aim. For Bob, it was the conformity and intellect-killing Subjective Aim of the fundamentalists that had to give way to the creativity that surged through every fibre of his being, calling him into his true humanity, to realize his potential in ways he had not yet dreamed.

Steven and Meg wanted to commit themselves to raising Audrey with a worldview that affirmed what they had come to know of the God of their experience, one that would not burden her with outdated theologies that could only limit her freedom, her creativity, her potential to bring novelty and joy in to the world. They wanted a ritual that affirmed their commitment to God's Initial Aim, rather than the deeply flawed Subjective Aim of a religious heirarchy.

Water, the primary element used in baptism, is a perfect symbol for the Initial Aim of the Spirit, because it bends to the will of no human being. In the words of the *Tao Te Ching*, it "is the softest thing in the world, yet there is nothing that can stand against it." Indeed, it can reduce mountains to rubble, it seeks out the low and unpopular places, and like the wind, it goes where it will.

The Initial Aim of God is like water. God is constantly whispering, constantly nudging. This nudging is easy to resist, but over time, through persistence and synchronistic circumstance, it can bend the will of the most stubborn actual occasion. Eventually, it will have its way. Eventually, the efforts of humankind to imprison, restrict, or codify the human spirit must fail.

The Initial Aim of God, the impulse toward freedom and creativity, will triumph.

What does baptism mean to you? If you were to undergo it today, what would you leave behind, and what would you embrace? What ideas, experiences, disappointments, or bondage would you wash away in that water? And when you rise forth from the water, what freedom, what creativity, and what new life do you desire to meet? In what way do you need to change? In what way do you need to say, "Yes!" to the nudging of God's Spirit today?

In the Catholic tradition, there is a "little baptism" that takes place every week, and in some monasteries, every day. It is a ritual of sprinkling holy water called the asperges, and its purpose is to remind us of our baptism and to renew our commitments to God and to one another.

Instead of the regular meditational prayer this morning, I would like to perform the ancient ritual of the asperges. This bowl contains holy water, and with this branch, traditionally a hyssop branch, I'd like to sprinkle you, lightly. So do cover up anything that shouldn't get wet.

Let us pause a moment to ask ourselves what it is that we leave behind, and what it is we most want to embrace.

*Dear friends,*
*this water will be used to remind us of our baptism,*
*of the waters that cleanse and make us new,*
*and of the waters of the Earth that refresh*
*and sustain all beings.*

*May God bless me as I perform this service.*
*With the Earth's hallowed waters do I*
*consecrate this holy altar and sanctuary.*
*And bless also this people*
*who gather to celebrate an astounding love.*
*Amen.*

From the Festival of the Holy Names liturgy.

*Confirmation is the rite in which*
*we express a mature commitment to Christ,*
*and receive strength from the Holy Spirit*
*through prayer and the laying on of hands*
*by a bishop.*

The Book of Common Prayer

# Chapter Eleven

## *Confirmation*

I didn't ask to be born a Christian. The fact that I wound up in a Christian family is an accident of the world's unfolding, just like the fact that I am male, a "creative type," or of Celtic ethnicity. Everything I am is the result of a roll of the cosmic dice. My parents might have been Hindus, or Jews, or even Baha'i's. But no, they were Southern Baptists, and so, therefore, was I.

Like a lot of people, though, I experienced the legalism of the Southern Baptist faith as deeply wounding, and as soon as I was out of high school, I rejected the faith of my parents. On the one hand I can see this as a sad thing, as Christianity—even Southern Baptist Christianity—has many valuable things to offer. It creates meaning, and provides tools and community that can guide and support in life-giving ways.

But religion is a powerful thing, and like all powerful things, it is dangerous. Ironically, religion as a phenomenon is morally neutral. A gun isn't evil, as the NRA is quick to point out, but people can choose to use it in either useful or harmful ways. Religion is no different.

The only way to heal from the wounding I experienced as a fundamentalist was to reject the Christian tradition altogether. It was a painful but necessary stage in my growth. I learned who I was, apart from who I was being *told* I was by dogma and tradition. I used this time to explore other religions, and tried on their ideas of who I was as I might hats at the haberdashery.

It was all very liberating and insightful, but eventually I had to acknowledge that the symbols and stories of the Christian tradition were deeply ingrained in my identity. They made me who I was, and although I could spend my life running from them, trying to shoehorn another symbol set into my psyche, why put myself through it? The Christian God was not going to go away, no matter how hard I tried or how far I ran— better to simply make peace with "him."

My salvation came in the form of the Episcopal Church. For in this place, I learned to hold all of the stories, symbols, and doctrines I had been taught as a child in radically new ways—ways that not only did not wound me, but that excited me, sparked my imagination, and gave me hope.

There I learned that God was not a bully in the sky, not just a dysfunctional father figure writ large, or a monster licking his lips in anticipation of my next screw-up, waiting to lower the Great Boom of Judgment. In the Episcopal Church, I met Jesus the Teacher of Wisdom. In the weekly pronouncement of the Gospel, I heard the Good News of God's love and promise for the very first time.

I had first been baptized at the age of eight. At the time, I was saying "yes" to the Christian faith of my childhood. Episcopalians honor the baptism of all Christian denominations and do not re-baptize people when they join the Episcopal Church. Instead, I chose to be confirmed in the Christian faith as I understood it as an adult.

Baptism and Confirmation have always been closely related sacraments. In the Eastern Orthodox church, it is simply part of the baptismal ritual. Baptism is the parents' promise to be faithful to God, or in the case of an adult baptism, the promise of that person to be faithful. Confirmation is God's covenant to be faithful to that person in turn, as that person is sealed with oil "as Christ's own forever."

In the West, however, the two halves of this ritual have been severed and are usually separated by as much as twelve or thirteen years. When a baby is baptized in the West, he or she is welcomed into the "ark" of the church, and a commitment is made by the parents and godparents to raise the child in the faith.

Confirmation usually takes place when a child has come of age, and is old enough to understand the subtleties of Christian doctrine and assume the responsibilities of the life of faith. At that time, a person may choose to affirm for him- or herself the baptismal covenant made on his or her behalf at baptism.

One can think of it as the world's longest sacrament, one that often takes thirteen years to complete! But instead, we in the West have opted to see it as a separate rite, at once a coming-of-age ritual, as well as an acknowledgement of a process begun many years ago.

Confirmation is thus a natural for the Process system of thought. It is not so much an end-point, a completion, as it is a public witness to the progressive unfolding of the life of faith for an actual occasion.

Whitehead speaks of processes happening by a series of positive or negative prehensions. When two occasions interact, if one takes away from that interaction something that changes it, it has positively prehended. If that interaction does not change either occasion, Whitehead calls this a negative prehension.

When I left the Baptist church and turned my back on the Christian faith, I negatively prehended it—I stopped interacting with it, I stopped allowing it to inform my life, I no longer allowed it to *change* me.

But when I discovered the Episcopal Church, I began to positively prehend the Christian tradition again. I acknowledged it, interacted with it, invited its wisdom, and underwent profound changes as it informed the process that is my life. In being confirmed, I publicly ritualized my positive prehension of the Christian faith and tradition.

In many ways, Confirmation does for liturgical Christians what Baptism does for Evangelical Christians—they are both rituals that acknowledge an adult commitment to the Christian life. One can also see Confirmation as analogous to the Evangelical practice of rededicating one's life to Christ. However, although a rededication can be done as often as desired, a person is confirmed only once.

Confirmation, for Process Christians, might be

called the Sacrament of Positive Prehension, acknowledging to all the life-giving power of Jesus' field of force.

By making such a public declaration of faith and commitment, one not only testifies to the life-giving power of the gospel, but one implicitly invites others to positively prehend it as well.

The ritual action associated with this Sacrament is chrism, the smearing of oil—otherwise known as anointing. In the ritual life of ancient Israel, oil was poured over the heads of those who were either ordained as prophets or enthroned as kings. The word "Messiah" is simply Hebrew for "that guy who had oil dumped on his head," or "anointed one." The Greek word, "Christ," means exactly the same thing. It is easy to see how the words "Christ" ("anointed") and Chrism ("oil") are related.

So the words "Messiah" or "Christ" were not always reserved for one person—any prophet or a king was a "messiah." In Christian confirmation, both the prophetic and royal connotations are present. As Christians, we believe we have been "adopted" into God's family—we are not servants of Jesus, nor even merely friends, but siblings. The royal status afforded the Sovereign of the Universe is, in the sacrament of Confirmation, bestowed upon us. It is, in effect, a coronation rite, in which we take our places as princes and princesses in the royal family, heirs to the unlimited potentiality of God's Primordial Nature.

That is the privileged aspect. But as everyone knows, with privilege comes responsibility. As members of Christ we are charged with the responsibility to proclaim the Truth, even when it is not popular. We do this when we stand up to injustice, when we speak out against evil, both personal and social, when we put ourselves in harm's way for the benefit of others. In this prophetic role, we must allow time for quiet. We must listen for the "still small voice" of the Spirit, which is always nudging us toward God's Initial Aim. Once we have discerned what the Spirit is saying, it is our responsibility as Christians to stand in our role as prophet and to boldly speak Truth so that others may clearly discern the Way of Life, the way of creativity and freedom, and may be given an opportunity to choose it.

As I stood with the other confirmands at St. John's Episcopal Church, I felt the weight of both of these rich and portentous meanings. One at a time we knelt before the bishop. He put oil on our heads, signifying to all that we, too, were "Christ," or "anointed ones." Then he gave our cheeks a light slap—a reminder that the Christian life was not all sweetness and light. It would be hard—and indeed, it is. But by positively prehending the deep and ancient wisdom of this path, we are made more than we were—indeed, we are made both princes and prophets.

*Jesus, thou art both prince of peace*
*and the mouthpiece of wisdom.*
*Help us, when we affirm for ourselves*
*the mysteries of this Christian journey,*
*to carry ourselves with the dignity*
*that is rightfully ours*
*as royal daughters and sons of God,*
*and give us discernment and courage to hear thy Truth,*
*and to speak it, even when it is hard.*

*For indeed, as members of thy church*
*we are members of thee,*
*not "Christians," but "Christs,"*
*possessing both privileges and responsibilities,*
*gratefully receiving the gift of this life,*
*and at the same time being gifts to the world. Amen.*

*The Holy Eucharist is the sacrament commanded by Christ for the continual remembrance of his life, death, and resurrection, until his coming again.*

Book of Common Prayer

# Chapter Twelve

## *The Eucharist*

One day Kate and I were watching the wonderful comedy film *Unstrung Heroes*, about a little boy's relationship with his, well, somewhat "odd" uncles. One of the "oddities" was the Jewish spirituality practiced by the uncles, which the child's parents, as "secular" Jews, dismissed out of hand.

After the movie, Kate turned to me almost in tears and said, "God, I love Jews!" I grinned and nodded, because I've often felt the same appreciation well up in myself. One of the things I enjoy most, besides giving us a deep and abiding spirituality which has molded our own faith, is the sense of humor that is almost stereotypical of the Jewish people.

Especially stereotypical is the image of the Jewish mother, hovering over her brood, and shouting "Eat! Eat!" every time they turn around. This is congruent with our image of a people who make great use of food for other things than simply bodily nourishment.

The Jews use a meal, for instance, to celebrate their liberation from Egypt in the Feast of the Passover, and a weekly meal on the Sabbath to celebrate God's gifts and faithfulness.

For the stereotypical Jewish mother, forcing food on her children is a way for her to demonstrate her love and care for her family. If her children are well-fed, she can be content that she has been a good mother.

With that in mind, I would like to suggest that we expand our repertoire of images for God with this one: God as a Jewish Mother. Now, we have prayed to God the Father for nearly two thousand years, but I believe there is room in our tradition for images that speak to us using a variety of metaphors, and since God as Mother is certainly a Biblical image, perhaps the idea of God as a "Jewish" mother is not so far off base.

So how does God fit the stereotype of the Jewish mother in our scriptures? We're used to thinking of the God of the Old Testament as being oppressively legalistic and thoroughly masculine. And yet, think back to God's nurture and care for the Israelites as they wandered in the wilderness for forty years. The Jews awoke every morning to find that God the Jewish Mother had provided all the food that several hundred thousand hungry pilgrims could possibly eat. And later, when they began to complain about the lack of variety, she sent more quail than they could cope with.

It isn't *just* food, of course, that God provides, but abundant food, prodigious food. In Isaiah 25:6-8, we read one of the most beautiful passages in scripture, and one that clearly pictures God providing a sumptuous feast for the whole of the earth:

"On this mountain God will make for all peoples a feast of rich food, a feast of well-aged wines, of rich food filled with marrow, of well-aged wines strained clear. And God will destroy on this mountain the shroud that is cast over all peoples, the sheet that is spread over all nations; he will swallow up death forever. Then God will wipe away the tears from all faces, and the disgrace of his people will be taken away from all the earth."

This is surely a maternal, nurturing, and feeding image, an image which transcends time and culture, a promise for people of various traditions. It provides us not only with a nurturing image of divinity, but also with a glimpse of what is surely part of God's Initial Aim, and a vision worth working for: the renewal of the earth, and the consummation of the present age of hunger, poverty, and injustice.

Not surprisingly, when Jesus appeared and began preaching about the Community of God, he also used food for his metaphors. To eat with someone was to embrace them, to approve of them; the opportunity to feed someone, to provide hospitality, was considered a great honor in New Testament Jewish culture.

Jesus, as part of this culture, not surprisingly adopted the images and metaphors that would be most meaningful to his people. So Jesus' first miracle was to provide wine at a party; Jesus' parables included a story about God as a man who threw a great feast, to which no one actually invited would go; and about God as the Jewish mother searching for her lost coins.

Mostly, however, he let his actions speak for themselves. For Jesus did not just dine with the "acceptable" people in society, but also spent his time dining with the kind of people no self-respecting Jew would be caught dead with: prostitutes, Roman collaborators, thieves, and political radicals. In Jesus' culture, they were outcasts—they lived outside the boundaries of "acceptable" behavior and thus put themselves beyond the reach of grace.

Whitehead speaks of nested fields of becoming, called "nexus." The acceptable people in Jesus' culture saw themselves as part of a nexus they called "the people of Israel," that was especially favored and graced by God. In their imaginations, those who lived "unacceptable" lives were no longer part of this nexus, this "people," and no longer shared in its benefits. But Jesus, in sharing a meal with such outcasts, said to them by his actions, "I approve of you, and not only that, God does, too." In the simple act of breaking bread with such "undesirables," he re-drew the boundaries of the "nexus of grace" that was thought to be favored by God. He drew it bigger than any of his fellow rabbis would have accepted. He drew it so big that no occasion was outside of it. In feeding the undesirables, in showing them love, respect, and acceptance, Jesus revealed God the Jewish Mother, bidding them all to partake of grace, to "Eat! Eat!"—and their lives changed forever.

Whitehead spoke of Jesus as generating a "field of force" that so powerfully impacted the world that its effects continue to reverberate through time, continue to impact the trajectory of the universe. It is amazing to think that such a powerful field of force was generated by such a simple act—the breaking of bread with friends. But that is how it happened, and how it continues to happen.

For Jesus is still inviting us to his table—he is still redrawing the circle of those who may dine at God's table larger than the so-called "spiritual authorities" are comfortable with. Every week we gather around Jesus' table and extend an invitation to any who would to take their place as equals, to receive an equal share of grace, no matter how "undesirable" people have been told they are, or believe themselves to be.

The meanings of the Eucharist have undergone many changes throughout the church's history. For many years, this meal has been seen as the instrument by which God converts us into Christ himself. In Whiteheadian terms, Jesus himself is a nexus, and when we positively prehend him, we join the evolving nexus that is Jesus. We join our loud voices to the quiet voice of the Spirit, calling the world back to God's Initial Aim of ever-increasing freedom, diversity, and creativity.

This is a powerful mystical theology which still has deep meaning for us today. Just how big is the nexus that is Jesus? According to Eastern Orthodox theology, the whole of the created order, the universe itself, is the nexus that is Jesus, and there is nothing, and no one, that is outside the circle of grace. All is in the process of divinization, a process that we are both made aware of and contribute to in the act of sharing bread with friends and strangers, with saints and sinners alike.

There are many, many mystical theologies of the Eucharist we could discuss, but it is sufficient here to say that even as Christians' needs have changed dramatically over the past two thousand years, the Eucharistic table has always been there to support them. Though the words, the actions, and even the meaning of the ritual have changed dramatically, the simple actions involved—the taking, breaking, and sharing of bread—have remained the same. People have been *fed*, both physically and spiritually.

And this is so because although cultures vary widely, people are basically the same. We need food. We need safety. We need guidance. We need love and support. And the symbols that best provide these things—a meal made sumptuous with rich wine, ornate vessels, and mysterious rituals—have come down to us through the centuries from the hands of an insightful rabbi named Jesus, who knew a good symbol when he saw it.

One of my favorite professors in college was Dr. Dana. She went to the same church I attended, and for her, it was not the words of the liturgy that impacted her, nor the ritual enacted by the priest. For her the most powerful element of the service was coming to the communion rail, kneeling, and holding out her hands.

For her, this simple action spoke volumes. It said, "I cannot do this alone. I need to receive sustenance from God." This simple action of holding out her hands spoke of her conscious dependence on God for her nourishment, indeed, for her very survival. The repetition of the rite from week to week spoke to her like the line from *Oliver*: "Please, sir, I want some more." But unlike the hard knocks given to poor Oliver, God—our Jewish mother—gives us exactly the nourishment we need.

*Eternal God,*
*from before the times of our reckoning,*
*we have celebrated with a holy meal*
*the family you have made of us.*
*You have come to us in many ways:*
*to the children of Abraham and Sarah,*
*you came in manna, the life-giving bread*
*that appeared as dew upon the ground,*
*nourishing and giving witness to your faithfulness*
*day after day.*
*To the disciples, you came in Jesus, the Bread of Life,*
*feeding the souls of all who have ears to hear;*
*to Christians you have come in the bread of Eucharist,*
*uniting a family of faith, now and forever more;*
*and to people of compassion everywhere*
*you have come in your life-giving Spirit*
*to provide a soulful feast for the whole of the Earth.*
*Therefore we ask that,*
*in the sharing of the bread at our table,*
*and in the drinking of the wine,*
*our own eyes might be opened to behold you*
*in the glory of your Creation,*
*in the Wisdom of your Word,*
*and in the faces of our sisters and brothers*
*gathered in your name to celebrate an astounding love.*
*Feed us now, God our Mother,*
*the things which we most need*
*to receive from your hand. Amen.*

Adapted from the Festival of the Holy Names liturgy.

*Holy Matrimony is Christian marriage,
in which the woman and man enter
into a life-long union, make their vows
before God and the Church, and receive
the grace and blessing of God to
help them fulfill their vows.*

The Book of Common Prayer

# Chapter Thirteen

## Marriage

One of the reasons I like weddings so much is that at the receptions I get to talk to teenagers. They are always intrigued by me, I think because I look so young, and they often will open up to me and talk about their struggles with religion, even if they wouldn't be caught dead talking to an "adult" about such things.

It was at the first wedding I ever performed, in fact, that one young woman confided to me that she was intending to leave Christianity and take up Buddhism. I told her that I thought Buddhism was a fine religion, and that she would probably learn a lot about herself; but why, I wondered, did she feel she had to leave Christianity? She told me at some length that she did not feel there was a place for her in her church, that the people felt cold and uncaring, that the things the church taught didn't have any meaning for her life, and finally that "ministers never listened to her."

"Well, I'm listening to you," I pointed out.

"Yes, but you don't count," she said. "You have earrings."

Now, although I was flattered at the street credibility my attire affords me, I was somewhat troubled by this young woman's dilemma. She is far from alone. Today, we see no lack of folks leaving their childhood faith and, as the prophet Hosea puts it in his book, "running off after foreign gods." It is no secret that the mainline churches are in desperate trouble. We are losing members at an alarming rate. Time and again, I have heard people like this young woman rail against the church as being irrelevant, sexist, or out of touch with reality. I do not blame them. They feel the same soul-aching hunger that every man or woman feels in their breasts, the same thirst for God, for some connection with the universe. And they are quite right that the church has not provided them with what they need to grow and to flourish in their spiritual lives. Not surprisingly, they go and chase after "foreign gods," exploring Sufism or Buddhism or some other exotic religion in a heartfelt and sincere search for meaningful spirituality.

Back when I was in college, my best friend was a marvelously creative fellow whom I'll call Mark in this sermon. After graduating, Mark met an attractive woman whom he apparently did not aggravate too much and they got married. A couple of years later, I got a collect phone call from him. Mark was in deep pain about his marriage and was considering leaving his wife.

I myself have been divorced and remarried, and as most of you know, my present marriage is not what you would call smooth sailing, so I think my experience gave me a bit of perspective on his dilemma.

I told him, "Listen, the issues you are dealing with here really have nothing to do with your marriage. You are both dealing with deep childhood wounds, and anytime you get into an intimate relationship, these same problems are going to surface. This is not about your wife, it's about you. And either you can deal with these issues now, or you can leave your wife, find someone else, and after the honeymoon is over you'll be in exactly the same place as you are now. These issues you are wrestling with are your shadow. They will follow you around your whole life and sabotage every relationship you have until you sit down and deal with them. So the questions you need to ask yourself are these:

1) Do I want to deal with these issues now or later?

2) Is my wife someone with whom I feel safe enough to work through my issues?

I don't know what kind of decision Mark made, because I haven't heard from him since that phone call. But the advice that I gave him has haunted me, especially when I think of the young woman I spoke to at the wedding reception. Rightfully dissatisfied with the religion of their birth, she and many, many of her generation leave their religion behind and go seeking after a God they can call "Mr. Right"—or "Mrs. Right," depending on the religion. But after five years, after the honeymoon, they find their new tradition to be just as sexist at its core, just as inflexible, just as corrupt as the church they left. The questions for them then become the same as those I put to Mark.

1) Do I want to deal with these issues now or later? Do I want to chase after yet another religion, or do I

want to work through my issues with my faith here and now?

2) Is the faith I am practicing now one in which I feel safe enough to work through my issues?

These are the real questions, friends. Not whether Buddhism is superior or inferior to Christianity, not whether one is right or the other wrong. But rather, is this a place that feels safe enough for you to ask the hard questions, to do the hard work, to wrestle with God as we all must do?

Harvill Hendrix is a brilliant marital counselor, who in his bestselling book *Getting the Love You Want* talks about what is really behind the difficulties couples face. He provides some startling revelations of what a couple has to do in order to work through their painful childhood issues.

Hendrix says that couples are attracted to one another because their partners embody the very elements of their parents that hurt them. A woman whose father was physically abusive is most likely to marry a man who treats her similarly. At the same time her abusive husband may be unconsciously attracted to this woman because she is submissive and unsupportive, just like his own mother. This is a pattern that is plain to see, especially if you are married. Hendrix's genius lies in the fact that he discerns a method to nature's madness: we enter into relationships to heal each other's wounds.

If my wife feels abandoned by her father, and I am the sort that runs from trouble, then every time we get into a fight and I go hide out somewhere, she feels the same stab of her father's abandonment. The only way that this wound can be healed is for me to stretch and grow beyond the behavior which hurts her. So when I am finally able to stay put even when we're fighting, the wound of constant abandonment in my wife can finally begin to heal.

Similarly if I was wounded by a hypercritical mother, then every time my wife makes a critique, my wound is opened all over again. But if my wife can stretch just a bit and learn to give me feedback which is not critical, then finally I can begin to heal.

Healing is sacred work. It is a mystery, and the Greek word *mysterion* is the very same one we use to translate into the English word "sacrament." The sacrament of Marriage exists for many good reasons, not the least of which is to provide safe and stable environments for the bearing and rearing of children. But marriage isn't only for the sake of children, it is also for the sake of the two people entering into the covenant. Marriage makes it hard to run. Marriage makes it difficult to just say, "I'm outta here," when the going gets rough. In short, marriage attempts to bind two people together long enough for them to heal.

There are more than two people involved in a marriage. There are three. There is one party, traditionally a man, and the other party, traditionally a woman, and then there is the person of the relationship they form. This "third man in the fire" must be nurtured and cared for as much as either of them individually. In Whiteheadian terms, these two occasions, who are themselves the nexus of many millions of occasions, come together to form a larger nexus that includes the two of them, but is itself a new occasion with a lifespan of its own.

And if this new person, this larger nexus, is properly cared for, it will most assuredly heal both of the original occasions that came of their own free will to be joined together.

In Christian tradition, the sacrament of marriage is symbolic of a larger and more significant relationship as well. Scripture is fond of using a love affair between a man and a woman as a metaphor for the relationship between the Divine and a beloved people. This metaphor is in evidence in both testaments. When God, the one party, woos human beings, the other party, a new nexus called Israel results. Likewise in the New Testament, Jesus is the bridegroom preparing the Wedding Feast of the Lamb for his Bride, his people, which forms another nexus, the church. In both cases, Israel and the Church are considered entities in their own right, "beings" that must be cared for and nurtured.

It is a good metaphor, and everything we have been saying about how marriage heals people applies here as well. Both God and humanity are in process, and in process *with each other.* This relationship has grown both parties immeasurably. History has not been kind to us, or to God. But in this romance, we both are given an opportunity to grow, and yes, to heal.

Some marriages are rocky, and so sometimes our relationships with the "third person," the nexus that results from a marriage, is not always felicitous. Our relationship with the nexus that is the church is very much like this. Many of us have been sorely wounded by our relationships with the church. And in turn the church has been sorely wounded by us, for it is we who make her what she is. How is it possible that the institution founded by Christ to be a healing balm in the world has been the cause of so much bloodshed, so much prejudice, so much intolerance? No wonder our children are running away! The church has hurt them, and we—by commission or omission—have hurt the church.

The answer is not to run away. The answer is not for us to give up on this marriage, or to go chasing after foreign gods. If the church has been hurt in the past by greed or intolerance, then we must stretch, we must change our behavior and heal her. There are countless thousands who have been hurt by the church's exclusivity, its sexism, its intolerance and rigidity. How do we heal them? We heal them by stretching, by changing our behavior so that their old buttons are no longer pushed, so that the abuse visited upon them in their formative years is not triggered or repeated.

Friends, the church is not a monolithic unchanging institution. It is a living entity, an ever-evolving, ever-growing personality with whom we all have a relationship—for many, a very painful relationship. But as Hosea testifies, running after foreign gods is not the answer. Examining, stretching, growing, and learning to love each other even when it's hard: this is the answer. This is the work we have to do. The wounds of spiritual abuse are deep in many, many people and they aren't going to just go away.

And so I leave you with these questions: Are we going to deal with these issues now or later? Is the church or the denomination we are in a place where we feel safe to work out our own issues? And even if you don't feel that you have ever been wounded by the church, are you willing to grow and stretch in order to heal those who have been? Are we going to be a balm for the suffering? This is our calling, and if we cannot answer in the affirmative, then we have no right to call ourselves "The Church."

*Holy and healing God,*
*our ancestors have not always been faithful to you.*
*We have not always been faithful to you.*
*As a result we have caused much pain,*
*our children have suffered for our limited vision,*
*and many have sought after foreign gods*
*because we have despoiled our home the church.*
*For many it is no longer a place of nurture,*
*of healing, of compassion, or liberation.*
*We are heartily sorry and we earnestly repent.*
*You have made us to be a light unto the nations,*
*and charged us to be your presence in this world.*
*Help us—and our children—not to flee from our pain,*
*but give us the strength of character*
*and the will to hang in there, to wrestle with you*
*and with the mighty issues that plague us,*
*that we may emerge from our struggles whole,*
*healed, and victorious as you intend your church to be.*
*Be near us in our meeting today, granting us*
*wisdom and compassion, and the grace to stretch,*
*to grow, and to heal one another. Amen.*

*Ordination is the rite in which God
gives authority and the grace of the Holy Spirit
to those being made bishops, priests, and deacons,
through prayer and the laying on
of hands by bishops.*

The Book of Common Prayer

# Chapter Fourteen

## *Ordination*

Our brother Lou is about to be ordained into the historic succession that stretches in an unbroken line from Jesus' hand to Bishop Charlie's. Kind of a scary thought, isn't it, Charlie? And yet that is the tradition that we keep alive, and to which we hold fast, and which we celebrate today with great joy. Each of us that have undergone this initiation have been charged with being a beacon on a hill, letting our light shine before others, to be salt, and to encourage saltiness in others.

But for too many people, the salt has lost its saltiness. The people whom Christ has charged to tend his flock have instead fleeced them, and there is much distrust of the clergy today. This is quite understandable, since for nearly two thousand years, the clergy have lifted themselves above the people they serve, have crafted of their sacred charge fiefdoms and dominions, and have rivaled secular kings and courts in their splendor and power. And many who serve smaller communities have, unfortunately, harbored pretentions to such power; others have become parodies of themselves. As a result of these abuses, we have lost much of our ability to season and to influence. Our light has nearly been snuffed out.

Today, Lou, you will make an oath of obedience to Bishop Charles, but your greater allegiance is obedience to Jesus. The Gospel of St. Luke recalls that the disciples were arguing amongst themselves over which was the greatest. But he said to them, "The kings of the Gentiles lord it over them, but it shall not be so with you; rather the greatest among you must become like the youngest, and the leader like one who serves."

Having the mind of a servant is not so hard when you are a deacon, as it is the role of a deacon to serve. But you will not be a deacon for long, and keeping the mind of a servant becomes more difficult when one becomes a priest, and more difficult still when one becomes a bishop. But if we are to be effective, it is this "servant-mind" that we must cultivate and cherish.

I have been very fortunate in my ministry to be given two communities in which I have learned this lesson the hard way. For about five years I had been privileged to organize a community called the Festival of the Holy Names. For many years the Festival met as a Eucharistic community on a weekly basis. Most of us had come from abusive religious backgrounds, and in the context of this new community, we hoped to discover what a healthy Christian community might feel like. Towards this end, we set goals for ourselves and developed guidelines that we held to tenaciously. First of all, we eschewed clericalism: we recognized no clergy. Either everyone was a priest when they stepped through those doors or no one was. Second, we wanted to be radically egalitarian: anyone who wanted to could sign up for a future service and say mass. Dogs and all other animals were welcome at God's table. Third, liturgies had to address the needs of all those assembled: every word, every line, every punctuation mark of every liturgy we used was open to discussion and revision at monthly planning meetings.

Now the Festival was largely my brainchild, and I had a definite vision for where I wanted it to go and what I wanted it to accomplish. Silly me. I very quickly discovered that my carefully crafted liturgies were replete with sexist and imperialistic assumptions I had been completely blind to. The Festival picked them apart mercilessly. My ego was crushed and my wife and I nearly divorced over the wording of a new Lord's Prayer. I kid you not.

But somehow God gave me the grace to persevere. I continued speaking my vision, putting my ideas and creativity out there, and about half the time, I got voted down. Now this was often discouraging, but in the end, it was the greatest blessing I could have received. For through this experience God taught me that being a real leader did not come through the exercise of power, but through assuming the roles of both prophet and servant. I had no power to wield in that community, and yet what I did possess was more than sufficient for the task: I had a vision, a voice to describe it, and one vote to help make it come about. But when the vote was

abz
Gethsemani Abbey
Morning Community Mass

taken, even if it did not go my way, I took it to mean that the Spirit had spoken, that my will and God's were not always the same, and that I still had much to learn.

I will forever be grateful for the gift of the Festival community, because it taught me what it meant to be a real leader. It is reported in one medieval Muslim manuscript that Jesus once said to his disciples, "If people appoint you as their head, be like their tails."

This is indeed the way of Jesus. St. Paul tells us that Christ "emptied himself of power and took the form of a servant." If we are to represent Christ, we must do no less. This is the true *imitatio Christi,* it is the way God does things. While both scripture and our imaginations are filled with nonsense about God as the all-powerful King in the sky who will strike "his" foes and bathe in their blood, our actual experience of God is very different. In Whitehead's Process Thought, God does not possess the power to strike anyone. There is no part of God, in fact, that is coercive. God has only the power to whisper, to suggest. Like myself in the Festival, God has a voice, and uses it, but we actual occasions often choose differently, and so the universe often ends up taking a crazy, circuitous route toward whatever it is becoming. It may not end up being exactly what God intended, but then, this is a collaborative project, and it may, in the end, wind up being a far more glorious—if weird—construction than even God could have foreseen or planned.

This is called "leading by following," and reminding you of its truth is the most precious gift I can think of to give you today. In the *Tao Te Ching,* the most sacred of Taoism's scriptures, the author is writing specifically to a young prince, teaching him how to be a leader. In poem 17, we read,

"The best leader is one that the people are barely aware of. The next best is one who is loved and praised by the people. Next comes one who is feared. Worst is one who is despised. If the leader does not have enough faith in the people, they will not have faith in him. The best leader puts great value in words and says little, so that when his work is finished the people all say, 'We did it ourselves!'"

Here at Grace North Church we fancy ourselves a "Congregational Catholic" parish. What this means is that while we worship in an Anglo-Catholic fashion, the parish is actually run by the parishioners. Day-to-day business is handled by an elected board, and major decisions are brought before the whole membership at quarterly parish meetings. As a result, the pastors have no administrative duties or responsibilities whatsover, and we are freed up to actually do our jobs: leading liturgy, visiting the sick, preaching, and teaching. We call this "political celibacy of the clergy," a phrase coined by my partner in crime here, Fr. Richard Mapplebeckpalmer. Although sometimes things move at a snail's pace as we wait for consensus, the result is that there is very little room for abuses of power. In this parish, at least, the clergy retain some of their saltiness.

That freedom extends both ways. For while the people are free to govern as they see fit, we clergy are free to speak the truth as we see it. There is nothing I can say from this pulpit which would, by itself, get me fired, and believe me, that is a freedom I have sorely tested over the years. What results from these tandem freedoms is a trust and appreciation between the people and their pastors which I have rarely seen.

Lou, as you are ordained into the historic succession today, you gain no magical powers, no hocus-pocus, no divine stamp of approval, no occult edge over the rest of humanity. What you gain is the trust of a community that extends mystically through time from the apostles to the present, and you gain the trust of a contemporary community of peers who say, "We see God's call in you, and we entrust ourselves to your care." The priesthood is not a monolithic institution, but an evolving entity to which you are joined in a conscious act of concrescence. You will change the priesthood, and the priesthood will change you as you commit yourself to this evolving process that is the apostolic succession.

It is an awesome and terrible responsibility. Jesus' most dire warnings are reserved for those who would deign to lead others spiritually. It is not a step to be taken lightly, but in full knowledge of what will be required of you.

For you do not commit yourself this day to a position of power or privilege, but one of servanthood, of listening, of leading by following, for very often the voice of the spirit will not be heard through you, and you must be listening for it in others. The wind blows where it will, and the Spirit will speak through anyone who listens. You have a vision, and you have a voice, and that light must shine on a hill, but if you try to force your vision, and if your voice drowns out the voices of others, that light will be dimmed. Today, you are salty, but if you abuse your position, you will lose the trust and respect of your people and your peers, and your saltiness, your effectiveness, your ability to season and influence will fade.

Today is a joyous occasion, but it is also one that requires sobriety and gravity. On behalf of all the ordained clergy here today, I embrace Lou as a brother in ministry, and rejoice in his election. Lou, in addition to the communities which you will lead, we clergy are also a community, and I hope and pray that you will call on us for the support you need as you find your sea legs as a deacon, and later as a priest. Charlie is your pastor, and we are your friends. Please lean on us, because no matter what you may face, it is likely that one of us has been there before you, and may have some helpful advice. You are not the lone ranger, you are a member of Christ's body, dependent on every other member. As you go forth to lead, remember that you must also follow. As you endeavor to be strong, remember that true strength requires vulnerability and humility. Above all, take heed of the words that Jesus spoke: "You are the salt of the earth—don't let that salt lose its flavor. You are the light of the world—don't let that light be dimmed. Instead, let your light shine before others, so that they may see your good works and give glory to your Father in heaven." Amen.

> *O mighty God, who are mighty in ways*
> *most of us would rather not fathom,*
> *relieve us of the fear of our own*
> *powerlessness and insignificance,*
> *that we might let you truly reign,*
> *by, of course, not reigning, as is your way.*
> *Help us to realize that it is*
> *only by dying that we truly live,*
> *it is only by relinquishing power*

*that we become truly powerful,*
*it is only by following that we become worthy leaders.*
*For we ask this in the name*
*of the one who washes our feet*
*and dries our tears,*
*our servant and yours, even Jesus Christ. Amen.*

Ordination Sermon for Lou A. Bordisso, January 26th, 2001.

*Reconciliation of a Penitent, or Penance,
is the rite in which those who repent
of their sins may confess them to God
in the presence of a priest, and receive
the assurance of pardon and the
grace of absolution.*

The Book of Common Prayer

# Chapter Fifteen

## *Confession*

When I was first ordained a deacon, my bishop told me to go get some experience by doing services in a nursing home. It was great advice. Nursing home folks are the most forgiving of congregations, because it doesn't matter how badly you screw up, they're just glad you're *there*. You could be the world's worst preacher, and they're just going to nod and smile and hope that they get a hug or can bend your ear privately for a moment before you go.

For the performer in me, it was also a captive audience. It was an instant congregation! They loved me, and I loved them. I recommend it to anyone just entering the ministry, as there is simply no better place to make your mistakes, pick yourself back up, and learn your chops.

The first nursing home I chaplained at was in Pleasant Hill, in an Alzheimer's Unit. There are certain

challenges to working with Alzheimer's patients. One is that they rarely remember who you are from week to week. Another is that they frequently think you are someone else.

I remember one woman, Gladys, who always thought I was her son, Jerry. One day I was standing with her and her daughter and son-in-law when she started manipulating something in the air that was visible only to her. "Help me with this, Jerry," she said to me. I had no idea what it was she was trying to do, and therefore no idea how to help. So I just stood there, looked at Glady's daughter, and shrugged. Finally, Gladys dropped her hands in exasperation and proclaimed, "Ah, Jerry, you're not worth a damn anyway." The situation seemed so absurd that I, her daughter, and her son-in-law all burst out laughing. Once we got going, Gladys joined in too, although a little uncertainly.

Once I was ordained a priest, I continued at the Alzheimer's Unit. It was rewarding work, and I had grown fond of many of the patients. Being a priest, the range of sacramental services I could offer expanded, and I brought them all to my work there. I began to say mass every Saturday, and I was able to hear confessions when people asked for it.

One gentleman did repeatedly. His name was Al, and he seemed to be absolutely consumed with guilt over something he had done in the far distant past. The first week he asked for it, I heard his confession and gave him absolution. He was relieved and grateful.

But as is often the case with Alzheimer's patients, his short-term memory was hopelessly impaired. He could remember the crime, but he could not remember being forgiven. So the next week, Al was back, asking me to hear his confession. I listened, and it was almost word for word, as if he had been rehearsing this for a very long time. Once again I have him absolution, and he tottered off, relieved.

The next week, he was back again. At first, this disturbed me, and I wondered if we were perhaps abusing the sacrament in some way. But when I spoke to my bishop about it, he told me to relax. God had forgiven Al long ago, but Al had not forgiven Al. It did no harm to remind him of his forgiveness, and if giving him the sacrament offered Al any comfort, then why in the world would I ever withhold it?

I remembered Al as I meditated on our Gospel reading this week. Here Jesus is, preaching to a packed house. And here are these four guys who know that if they can just get their friend close enough to Jesus the master would heal him. How to do it, though, with all those people around? Their solution smacks of a sitcom contrivance: why, just cut a hole in the roof and lower him down!

But the outcome is void of any madcap antics. They cut the hole, they lower their friend, and Jesus is amazed at their faith. He also sees that what keeps the man lame isn't a physical malady, but a psychological or a spiritual one. In order to rid him of his suffering, Jesus tells him that his sins are forgiven.

You can set your clock by the reactions of the religious leaders in the room. "Who does he think he is, assuming he has the power to forgive sins?" Mark, the author of this account, has a theological agenda to push, so he affirms Jesus' power to do just that.

But I'd like to suggest another interpretation that seems to be much more in line with Jesus' actual teaching about sin, redemption, and the Process nature of God. I'd like to suggest that Jesus told the man his sins were forgiven because they already were. I don't think Jesus waved his magic wand and made the man's sins disappear. I think he was telling the man what the truth has been all along: God understands how hard it is to be human, and he doesn't hold anything against you. He never has. God does not blame you for the mistakes you've made in your life, for the people you have hurt when you have been reacting out of your own pain. God loves you *as you are.*

People have spun their wild theologies and theories about who Jesus is and what he taught for centuries, but my friends, *this* is the good news. We don't need anyone to grant us forgiveness. We don't need a sacrament to wipe our slate clean, we don't need Jesus to die to slake God's bloodlust over our sin. We don't need any hierarchical church doling out grace to those they deem deserving. We don't need to pray any magical formula to get "saved." None of that is good news. All of it is, in fact, very bad news. And it's not what Jesus was about.

This is what he was about—he came to teach us what God is like, to tell us this very simple message: God loves you and accepts you just as you are. You don't need to do anything to be forgiven. The God of the Process Universe is not "making a list of who's naughty and nice" like some primordial Santa Clause. Whitehead's God is always rolling with the punches, is always saying, "Okay, so we start *here*." This God does not hold anything against you. Your slate is clean. You are really and truly and radically *free*.

The problem is, of course, that we are not free. But it is not God that is sitting up there with a tally of our rights and wrongs. It's us. We're the ones keeping track of our virtues and failures, all faithfully stored right up here, in our heads. We are trapped in the prison of our own shame, and it is this that keeps us from living the abundant life that Jesus calls us to.

So why is there the sacrament of confession at all? Why do we, week after week, publicly confess our trespasses and receive the general absolution? Not because we need God to forgive us, but because psychologically, *we need to hear that we are forgiven.* And we need to hear it often, because our memories are short, because we screw up much more than we want to, because we are insecure and so desperately in need of grace and love, commodities in such short supply in the big bad world out there. And so we come here to get it, among our friends, where we can be held in love and told again and again that everything is all right, and that, ultimately, "all shall be well."

We are just like that man in the nursing home, whose sins haunted him day and night, and whose Alzheimer's robbed him of the comfort of forgiveness and assurance. We all have Alzheimer's, in a sense. We all forget that God does not judge the way the world does, the way our parents did, the way we judge ourselves. Every week, we need to be reminded. Every week we need to be held by our friends and loved.

This week, when we exchange the peace, let's go a step further. Instead of simply saying, "peace be with you," look into your neighbor's eyes and remind them that all shall be well. Because we all need to be reminded. Because the Good News of Jesus is good news indeed. No one holds anything against you except you. And if you are willing, you can let even that go.

*Jesus, you taught us that whatsoever things*
*we bind on earth will be bound in heaven,*
*and whatsoever we loose on earth*
*will be loosed in heaven.*
*And indeed, we enter our next life burdened*
*only by those things we have not let go of in this.*
*Help us to forgive ourselves,*
*even as we have been forgiven by you,*
*so that when we meet our reward,*
*we will do it with arms empty of earthly baggage.*
*For we ask this in your name,*
*you who taught us that our sins*
*are already forgiven. Amen.*

*Unction is the rite of anointing the sick with oil,*
*or the laying on of hands, by which God's grace is*
*given for the healing of spirit, mind, and body.*

The Book of Common Prayer

# Chapter Sixteen

## Unction

Several months ago, a terrible event occurred to Gail, a friend of mine. She was dining at the Berkeley City Club with her husband of over fifty years when he quite suddenly fell very ill. They rushed him to the hospital, and shortly thereafter, he died. His aorta had ruptured without any warning, and there was nothing the doctors could do to save him.

Gail and I are in the same peer supervision group for spiritual directors. I found out about her husband's death because Nancy, another of our group, had called with the news. "Make sure you call Gail right now," she said. I muttered some kind of response that I don't recall and hung up. Then I froze.

I stood motionless for some time trying to sort out the mixture of feelings coming over me. On the one hand I was very sad. Gail's husband Saul was elderly, certainly, but I had observed that he was also one of those folks that seems to always be buzzing, always working on some project, always busy. It seemed doubly sad that someone so able, so active, should be cut down before his time. I felt deeply for Gail and wanted to comfort her.

On the other hand, I am aware that I am a very peripheral person in her life. More than an acquaintance, less than a close friend. I feared intruding by calling her at such a sensitive time. Why should her mourning be disturbed with a phone call from this person she barely knows? How insensitive is that? In the moment I felt the best thing to do was to simply give her space and offer my condolences at what I imagined would be a more convenient time.

In our subsequent peer group meetings, it became painfully clear to me how lonely Gail was, how desperate for a comforting word. It also became very clear to me that I had failed her by not calling her immediately, by not showing up, even though it seemed to me that I had very little to offer her in her grief.

I had learned some kind of lesson, but apparently not too well. Because shortly after this, our own beloved Conrad died. I had visited him not long before, and was profoundly uncomfortable. For I felt that we should be talking about his fears, his feelings about his approaching death, or other unresolved issues. I thought that I should be anointing him for healing, but instead we talked about what it would be like to live in Europe. If he had not been dying, I would have felt that it was a most appropriate pastoral visit. But as it was, I drove home feeling a little sick, and a lot like a failure. I had not been able to steer the conversation towards what I considered an "appropriate" topic, and felt ashamed that we had focused so much on me in our talk.

I was stricken with grief when I heard he had died. I felt I had failed him, and cocooned myself in my own sadness. What I ended up doing was failing Beth even worse in not being present for her. I thank God Father Richard was there, who seems to be so much more skilled than I in such occasions of extremity. In my rationalizations, I told myself that that is why Richard makes the "big bucks" around here, why he is the full-time priest, instead of me. It is true that I work pretty much full time outside the parish, and that Richard handles most of the visitation work. But I could not kid myself—I had let Beth down in a very big way, and I suspected that I had probably let Conrad down, too.

I then thought of all the parishioners who had died in the past several years, and how I might have been a better pastor to them. I sank into a pretty severe depression.

Then I realized that I had a choice. I could either slit my own wrists, or I could try to correct the problem.

I am happy to report that I chose the latter option, and realized that—"Doh!"—I have had absolutely no training in death and dying! What I needed was to take a class, to get some education in the subject. It was with some relief that I realized that ignorance is not the same as malfeasance. I resolved to get some training.

The first thing I did was to go to the Graduate Theological Union's website to look for a class. Unfortunately, there was nothing. I was amazed, incredulous. How could there *not* be a class on this? I sent some emails out to some friends with connections at the seminaries and asked them for help.

One friend suggested that I call a man named Dave, the Dean of the Lutheran seminary, and ask his advice. I did so, and he regretted that he knew of no such courses. In fact, in the pastoral care class that he taught, there was only a single three-hour session devoted to death and grieving. But perhaps feeling bad that he did not have more to offer me, he invited me to come by for a visit. I thanked him and agreed.

When we met, I liked him immediately. He bade me get comfortable, and then we dove into the subject. I told him much of what I have just told you, and asserted that if there were just a class, some guidelines that would tell me what it is I am supposed to say, how I am supposed to act, perhaps I wouldn't be such a clueless failure as a pastor. I told him that I was pretty much an agnostic and couldn't stomach spouting platitudes or promises of some mythical afterlife. And short of that, I just didn't know what to *do*.

Dave was very kind, and said he understood my dilemma. Then he asked me a simple question that I should have seen coming, but didn't. "What if you had just come from the doctor where you were told you only had a month to live? Your pastor is coming for a visit. What do you want him to say? What do you want him to do?"

I grabbed the Kleenex box because I was beginning to lose my composure. "I don't think I would want him to say much," I told him. "I think I would just want him to hold me while we cried together."

He nodded. "So why don't you do *that*?" After I had absorbed this, he elaborated. "There really isn't much *to* say. The best thing we clergy can do is just be there. We don't need to spout platitudes, people don't want that. They don't want pie-in-the-sky stories about heaven, either. Mostly, they just don't want to be alone, and they want to know they are loved."

In the sacramental tradition of the church, we bring to the sick and dying the sacrament of unction, the anointing with oil for healing. We pray for them, we lay on hands, we smear a bit of olive oil. I used to think it was a bit of a silly sacrament. I don't really believe in miracles. I don't think someone is going to really get any better if I pray for them. God will do what God will do, and I have very little influence in the matter.

But after my meeting with Dave, I understood this sacrament in a very different way. There's really no priestcraft involved. No hocus-pocus, nothing magical about the application of oil. But there is something magical about the touch of another person. There is something warm and comforting about the feel of oil on one's skin. There is a solidarity in praying together that is, indeed, a healing thing. Unction isn't a sacrament only priests can perform, but it is one we ought to perform at every opportunity. The real unction, the real healing is not in the application of oil, but in the human presence offered to one who feels frightened and alone. The real healing comes from holding someone while we both cry. Real healing comes from meeting the painful reality head-on, but not having to do it alone.

For God is present in that holy meeting. In every instance of it we see the pieta, the wounded and the mourning locked in anguished embrace before God. Christ is both the wounded and the mourner. Christ is present every time we leave our fears and insecurities and pretenses and masks at the door and are really and truly present for what is really happening to the people we love. Apparently, like most other occupations, success in ministry is 96% just showing up.

In the Process universe, God does not really have the power to intervene, to heal in the extraordinary ways that we like to think God can. Instead, all beings have free will. Rocks and stars have what free will rocks and stars can exercise. The human body, that nexus of billions of smaller occasions, has free will, as do each of those billions of occasions. And when that nexus and each of those occasions feels loved and cared for, feels that fighting for life is worth it, they are much more likely to choose that life, to choose to heal, on whatever microscopic or macrocosmic level we care to consider.

Like most sacraments, Unction is symbolic. It necessitates actually being there. It necessitates concern and care, represented by touch—and it is in that touch that healing is found. Its symbol is oil, which soothes the skin as much as the sacrament soothes the emotions and the soul. For those who can receive it, it is the positive prehension of love and care, of both human and divine solidarity. For those who are unconscious, it is a reminder to those of us who apply the oil that love and concern don't require appreciation to be given. Grace is free.

It's not, of course. As I know so painfully well, showing up and offering that grace is some of the hardest work I have ever done. Yet I do not need to be anything other than what I am to do that work. I do not need to show up with all the answers, or with profound words of comfort. I just need to show up, complete with all my warts, fears, insecurities, and unruly emotions. I just need to be there, with ready arms and a little flask of oil. The gospel has always been about wholeness, after all. If I cannot show up as a whole person as your priest, what good am I to you who are also striving for wholeness?

In the incarnation, Jesus gives us a pattern for ministry that has long gone ignored. Jesus did not come in glory and power; he did not, as the *Gospel of John* might have us believe, have all the answers and raise himself up as the answer to all the world's questions. And it will do us no good, as ministers in his name, to try to do this now. Instead, Jesus came to us as a vulnerable and fallible human being, full of his own insecurities and hurt, who screwed up now and then, who often did not know exactly what to say.

The Pauline tradition has tried to paper over the cracks in Jesus' character, but they are plain to see for anyone who cares to look. From his failure to come when his friend Lazarus needed him, to his anguish in the garden, Jesus was far from the perfect messiah. And yet, in all of his humanness, he showed up, and he stayed with his friends until the end. He was not perfect, but he was whole, and he was present with his whole being, strengths and weaknesses alike. And it was *this* that brought the healing. Not the oil, not any magic words. Just *presence*.

A couple of weeks ago, I received Richard's email that Harriet had died. Once again, I felt lost in a vertigo of thoughts—I shouldn't bother Jim, maybe Richard is there, I don't know what to say, I have no comfort to offer. "Knock it off, dammit!" I told myself and picked up the phone. As I dialed I said a prayer that God would give me the right words. Jim didn't pick up the phone, but it was quickly passed to him. I told him I had just heard about Harriet. I told him I was so, so sorry, and asked if there was anything I could do. "I'm just glad you called, Johnny," Jim said. "Thank you." I told him I would be praying for Harriet's soul, and for him and his family. I told him to please give me a call if there was anything I could do. Then I hung up the phone and wept. It wasn't Unction, exactly, but it was close.

I still don't know what to say. I still struggle with conflict-avoidance, not wanting to involve myself where emotions are high. I still don't have any answers. And I am still going to screw this up on occasion. But I have learned something very dear, even if I'm not sure exactly how to live it out. All I really have to do is show up. Maybe that's enough for all of us.

*Eternal God of love and power,*
*we give thanks for Jesus,*
*who showed us how to minister*
*to one another with his whole being.*
*He came to us not as a god, but as a human being,*
*not in power, but in weakness,*
*not invincible, but vulnerable,*
*not perfect, but fallible and uncertain.*

*We rejoice that we are his body on earth now,*
*and it is sometimes a frightening prospect,*
*for we feel like we should be more than we are.*
*Yet you do not ask perfection of us, but only wholeness.*
*Help us to show up with all that we are,*
*to rest in our own integrity,*
*to embrace ourselves even as you embrace us in love.*
*And help us to bring that love and acceptance*
*to all that we meet.*
*Jesus, we know that you have*
*no hands on earth but ours,*
*and that they are just as feeble*
*and willing as your own were.*
*Save us from our own pretensions,*
*save us from our own fears,*
*for your name's sake. Amen.*

# PART FOUR

# Being Christian,
# Being Real

What makes you a Christian? When I was growing up, I would have told you that you are a Christian based on what you *believe*. But this kind of thinking would be alien to the Jews. Jews are Jews until they die. Regardless of what they believe, they are part of the family.

Christianity, however, is not an ethnic religion; we can't belong by birth. But I suggest that it is still not what we believe that make us Christians. The myth of unity of belief amongst Christians is, as we have seen, no longer tenable. No two Christians believe exactly the same thing. There are, in fact as many Christianities as there are practicing Christians.

Belief and Blood are not options for us. Fortunately, Process Thought provides us with a workable model. Process Thought, as an action-based philosophy, teaches us that we are Christians because we follow Jesus. "Follow" is a verb. It does not imply intellectual thought, but movement. It does not imply assent, but action. The earliest of Christians held wildly divergent beliefs from one another. What made them all

Christians is that each, to the best of their ability, sought to live as they believed Jesus would have them live.

A couple of months ago, while researching a story for the *Pacific Church News*, the magazine of the Episcopal Diocese of California, I visited a Spirituality-At-Work meeting in the cafeteria of a busy San Francisco office building. Here about six people of faith met over their sandwiches to pray together and talk about living spiritually in the workaday world. During one point in the conversation, the participants seemed to grope for a way to assess that day's spiritual "success." Leave it to business people to want to count out their spiritual till at the end of the workday!

During a pregnant pause, I was reminded of the prophet Micah's exhortation of the people of Israel: You have been told what is good. You know what God requires of you: to act justly, to love mercy, and to walk humbly with your God. I spoke this verse to the group and heads nodded in assent all around.

Here it was: simple, elegant, all-encompassing. Here is what God requires of you. Here is how you may gauge how "successful" you have been in your spiritual life this day. Theologians may spin their theologies from here to kingdom come, but when we bring our heads out of the clouds, and feel our feet once more on the good earth, we come back to the same three things: act justly, love mercy, walk humbly with God. These aren't beliefs, they are *actions*. A truly Process Christianity is not concerned with how we think, or with any of the illusory "things" or structures upon which we hang our faith. We are Christians only because of what we *do*.

There is great wisdom in Micah's exhortation—he knew what he was talking about. In some ways, his situation was similar to our own. The children of Israel had been taken away into captivity in Babylon. Judah had been conquered and colonized. The religious ideas of the Jews were being challenged by their proximity to their Zoroastrian neighbors, and there was no little bit of religious uncertainty and confusion. Micah warned them about the dangers of tossing away their heritage and reminded them that God really only requires very little.

Just as in a time of great personal stress, my three post-modern doctrines (described in Chapter One) made sense of my existential discomfort, likewise in another time of great stress, it was these three doctrines of Micah's that comforted and supported this great people of faith. I believe they can comfort and support us as well.

*You have been told, O mortal, what is good;*
*and what does God require of you*
*but to* DO JUSTICE, *and to love kindness,*
*and to walk humbly with your God?*

Micah 6:8

# Chapter Seventeen

## *Do Justice*

Over the holidays, I found that every time I passed the Oakland Airport on 880 towards my new home, I would glance at a sign off to the right, but too late. I say too late, because it is the type of sign that has huge words the size of minivans spelled out by a grid of lightbulbs. The sign is always changing, in a regular, rotating pattern. Even banks have these kinds of signs, rotating from the temperature to the time to an ad about their interest rates.

This sign, however, is situated atop a labor union building, and every time I saw it, it said in enormous letters "NO PEACE." What a disconcerting message. What did it mean? I realized that it was probably the tail end of a longer message, the first part of which I was not able to catch simply because I have impeccably bad timing. One day I was resolute and watched the sign deliberately, not waiting for it to simply catch my eye, and I finally saw the first part of the message: "No justice."

"No justice. No peace," was the full message. It was powerful. It was also familiar, being a condensation of the Roman Catholic peace and justice movement's famous dictum: "If you want peace, work for justice."

This is not a liberal catch-phrase. It is not the rallying cry of leftist or socialist rabble-rousers. It is a simply stated truth. If there is no justice, there can be no peace.

Think about that for a minute. If a government, such as El Salvador's, denies its people justice, especially its poorest people, they will be resentful and troublesome. Perhaps, like the American colonies suffering under the injustice of George the Third, the people will take up arms and declare war. No. Unless there is justice in the land, peace will not follow.

In our own country, it was an entire population of African-Americans who decided they were fed up with the injustice they suffered at the hands of white Americans. Though they did not make war, they denied the possibility of peace until justice was awarded them.

What about on a smaller scale? In our daily lives it is no different. If we treat our neighbor unfairly, he is likely to yell at us, punch us in the nose, or sue us. If we treat our spouse badly, our domestic lives are likely to turn into a living hell. If we are cruel and authoritarian with our children they will rebel and crush any sense of peace within our family. Does the fault lie with the child, with the spouse, or with the neighbor? Certainly not. It is a case of simple causality.

What about on a global scale? According to the Gaia Principle, a recent variation of Process Thought, unless we wake up and view the earth as a living organism, with needs and rights to be protected, we are in grave trouble. If we destroy the only means of support we have, we incur famine, disease, and death on a scale we can scarcely even imagine, unparalleled in the entire history of humankind. Justice for the people must include justice for the earth, or the people will have no place to enjoy their peace.

It is a simple concept, but it is difficult to really bring home. If, in your everyday life, you know strife, this strife was probably precipitated by some act, knowingly or unknowingly, of injustice. We are all guilty of it. Instead of hearing out our neighbor's grievance, we write them off as crazy. Instead of listening when someone says that we have hurt their feelings, we brush it off, or blame it on them.

Truly listening to one another is a great spiritual discipline. It is one which we consciously strive to engender in this community. It is also a discipline at which we frequently fail. It doesn't mean we don't, or shouldn't try; it just means we are human. But it is also human to pick ourselves up when we fall and try again. I am proud that we in this community seek to listen, that we know how to brush the dust off of our butts, and also that we know how to forgive each other.

But spiritual discipline also involves attention, bringing our awareness into ever more remote areas of our lives. In this, the Process God is our partner. We are growing into greater consciousness, greater sensitivity, and greater receptivity to the Spirit. This doesn't happen overnight—it's a process. It is a lifetime's journey. It started the moment you emerged howling from the womb and begins afresh each morning when your feet hit the rug at the side of your bed.

I do not think we need to be sign-carrying protesters shouting for "justice!" Although public demonstrations are important and have their place, most of us desire quieter lives than this. The challenge for us is to listen to the still, small voice of God in our breasts, who is not shouting "Justice!" but instead is whispering, "Were you fair to your brother? Did you hurt your sister's feelings?" And then there is the subtle nagging of the Holy Ghost, reminding you that there will be no peace until you make it right.

We do not like to be reminded of our sin. We have inherited too much of the Puritan mindset that put the scarlet letter "A" on the clothing of adulterers, and proclaimed that their lives were defined by and limited to this sin.

But we are much more than our sin. We are beings of infinite worth, of marvelous construction, capable of sublime beauty and meaning. *And we all blow it.* We have the power to sin and the power to repent; the power to hurt and the power to heal; the power to offend and the power to say "I'm sorry." We have the power to make justice and the power to make peace. And, as Mechtild of Magdeburg said in the 14th century, "God has given us the power to change our ways."

> *Holy Spirit, you who whisper*
> *to each and every one of us, day after day,*
> *help us to listen to your gentle nudges,*
> *help us to heed your warning*
> *when we have acted selfishly,*

*or have even unknowingly hurt someone we love.*
*Give us compassion for those whom we do not know,*
*and yet who are affected by our actions.*
*Help us to be conscious, and to be agents of your justice*
*in the world around us, private and public,*
*in big arenas and small.*
*For only then will the planet know peace,*
*and only then will our hearts know it, too. Amen.*

*You have been told, O mortal, what is good;*
*and what does God require of you*
*but to do justice, and to* LOVE KINDNESS,
*and to walk humbly with your God?*

Micah 6:8

# Chapter Eighteen

## *Love Kindness*

There is a cliché in our culture that I wish were not so true: No good deed goes unpunished. It probably would not have survived as a saying if it were not truth. Recently, as Kate and I were getting settled into our new house, I was determined to get pictures on the wall and to put things in their places as soon as possible, so that we would feel at home as quickly as we could.

Kate had hung up in the kitchen a small calendar that I took to be one of those toss-away freebies given out by the drug store. So when I was browsing around in Mazel Tov, the Jewish bookstore in San Francisco, I found a beautiful, oversized wall calendar filled with full-color reprints of medieval Jewish manuscripts from the British Library. When I got home, I tossed the little cheepo calendar and proudly hung the gorgeous calendar filled with Judaic antiquities in the kitchen.

I was proud of my find and imagined Kate squealing with delight when she stepped through the door. So you can see why, when she finally did get home and walked into the kitchen, I was shocked and horrified when she pointed to my new beautiful calendar and exclaimed, "What is *that*?! What did you do with my gardening calendar??!"

I was taken aback, "Your what?" I asked.

"My gardening calendar," she said angrily, "The one Kelly gave me as a housewarming present."

As you can imagine, I was casting around for an appropriately sized rock to hide under. Finally I gave up the search and went poking around in the recycling bin for the calendar, which was safe and sound. Looking at it closely, I saw that it wasn't cheap, just small, and beautifully illustrated with many different English gardens.

Of course, when I explained to Kate that I thought it was a throwaway, she was still feeling a little hurt, but she understood that I thought I was doing something sweet, something to make our home feel warmer and more like "us."

Kate did eventually appreciate the gesture, dappled as it was. My intentions were pure, and this is what, in the end, really mattered. In the end, the thoughtfulness won out over the thoughtlessness—thank goodness for me!

Now, although this is a story about kindness gone awry, it is about kindness, nonetheless. Kindness is something of a disparaged notion in our culture. In youth culture, it is especially obvious. Kids are likelier to revere someone for their toughness than for their tenderness. When a bunch of teenagers sees someone they admire coming towards them, they are much more likely to say "He's bad!" than to say "He's kind!" Kindness is not a badge of honor in our dog-eat-dog business culture either. I wouldn't say that kindness has gotten a bad rap, but I would say that it has been "dissed," to use the modern vernacular. Lots of lip-service may be paid to the idea in the classroom or on the Barney the Dinosaur show, but actually "doing" kindness out where people can see you? Let's just say that kindness is not likely to buy you much street credibility.

In the last chapter's discussion of justice, I made the point that it is not, in the end, what we believe or what we say that matters. It is what we do. Micah's admonition begins with acts of justice, and then quickly balances this with acts of mercy, or lovingkindness.

The Hebrew word for lovingkindness in Micah's verse is "Kheh'-sed" which means "kindness, lovingkindness, merciful-kindness." It is not so much a state of mind as it is a spiritual discipline, to be acted upon on a daily basis.

Our Jewish forebears were very perceptive. They knew well that what we say is often not congruent with what we do, and moving the people from words to action was an important emphasis in their spirituality.

To give you an idea of just how important this concept of lovingkindess was to them, I'd like to tell you a story from the Talmud:

Once Rabban Yohanan ben Zakkai was leaving Jerusalem, and his student Rabbi Joshua followed him. Seeing the Temple in ruins, Rabbi Joshua said: "Woe are

we! For we see in ruins the place where Israel's sins could be atoned for!" Then Rabban Yohanan told him: "Be not upset, my son. There is another way of gaining atonement that is just as effective. That is: deeds of lovingkindness. For it is written, 'I desire lovingkindness, not sacrifice.'"

This is an amazing reading, because it elevates the act of kindness to having the same cosmic efficacy as the fire of sacrifice. Now on the one hand, you could brush this reading aside and say, "Well, the Romans destroyed the temple in 70 CE. The Jews had to justify their continued existence somehow. They had to deal with their sins in some fashion."

But think of all the ways the need for atonement could have been fulfilled. It could have been filled by meditation, as in India where meditation, or internal, mental sacrifice supplanted the earlier practice of the Fire Sacrifice. Or by obedience, a sacrifice of the will upon the altar of the heart, as in Islam. Or a sacrifice of fasting, as so many faiths do.

But no. The Jews replaced sacrificial atonement with a sort of atonement that brings its own blessing: acts of love and kindness.

Now this was quite a switch. It traded the vertical sacrificial relationship between God and humanity and laid it down horizontally. Now atonement would come not by what we do for God, but what we do for our brothers and sisters—even for total strangers—what we do for each other, and what we do for the earth. Instead of erecting another barrier, another altar to separate God and humankind, the theology of lovingkindness brought God into the milieu of everyday human life.

This shift in consciousness was already underway

before the temple's destruction. Already the center of Jewish worship was beginning to change from the Temple in the heart of Jerusalem to the synagogue in the heart of the community. This gradual change in attitude would make it possible for another insightful rabbi to say, "Whatever you do for the least of these, you do to me." God is there in the midst of us.

The Talmud tells us that Rabbi Elazar, expounding upon the story about Rabbi Yohanan and the temple, told his students that "Deeds of lovingkindness are superior to charity in three respects. Charity can be accomplished only with money; deeds of lovingkindness can be accomplished through personal involvement as well as with money. Charity can be given only to the poor; deeds of lovingkindness can be done for both rich and poor. Charity applies only to the living; deeds of lovingkindness apply to both the living and the dead."

Rabbi Elazar is telling us that just giving money doesn't do it. We have to get our hands dirty. We have to get busy; we have to do it *ourselves*. Charity will not save us from our own sin, but lovingkindness will. That's a lot to think about.

As I suggested, this concept has its place deep in the teaching of Jesus. The earliest testimony of Christians taught that it was Jesus' mission to call Israel to cease sacrificing; that his tirades in the temple were against the sacrifices themselves. This tradition said that Jesus' message was that obedience and kindness were more important than the shedding of blood. He predicted the Temple's demise, which indeed took place less than one generation after Jesus' death.

Jesus' own teachings about atonement, and especially judgment, concur. In the Sermon on the Mount, Jesus tells the crowd about Judgment Day, about the sheep and the goats, the bliss of eternal life, the gnashing of teeth in outer darkness. I'd like us to look at the criteria for salvation in this reading. Are the sheep those who offered the appropriate sacrifices? Are the sheep those who "followed the rules" and kept the law perfectly? Are the sheep those who embrace the correct "statement of faith"?

No. Jesus says, 'Come... inherit the kingdom prepared for you from the foundation of the world; for I was hungry and you gave me food, I was thirsty and you gave me something to drink, I was a stranger and you welcomed me, I was naked and you gave me clothing, I was sick and you took care of me, I was in prison and you visited me.'

According to this tradition, it is not following the rules that is going to count at Judgment Day. It is not whether or not one has made the appropriate sacrifices. It is not whether or not one embraces the "proper" teachings. It's much more simple than that. Jesus is not going to ask us about any of these things. Instead, Jesus is going to ask us about our kindness. Did we give food to the hungry, water to the thirsty, hospitality to the stranger, nurture to the ill, companionship to the lonely? This, according to Jesus, is going to be our only defense at Judgment Day.

Perhaps we are going to be asked to give an account of the kindness we offered to strangers, or to our enemies. I hope we will have some stories to tell. For it is only in how we love one another that we demonstrate in any meaningful way how we love God. As the great

Process Theologian Teilhard de Chardin wrote, "Up until now, to adore has meant to prefer God to things by referring them to God and by sacrificing them to God. Now adoration means the giving of our body and soul to creative activity, joining that activity to God to bring the world to fulfillment by effort and intellectual exploration" (*Meditations with Teilhard de Chardin* [Santa Fe: Bear and Company, 1988], p. 129).

My mother had great admiration for a man whom she did not understand at all. Albert Schweitzer was a brilliant theologian, a talented organist, and a notorious heretic. Schweitzer was a Unitarian who rejected the idea of Jesus' divinity, and any notion of the vicarious atonement. He was a heathen of the highest order. He did not believe the "right" things about Jesus, and was therefore, according to my mother, "on the devil's highway."

And so because of this, my mother could only shake her head in bewilderment when she told me how this heathen had given up everything he had to practice medicine amongst the poorest of the poor in Africa. And the most troubling piece of information? That Schweitzer said he had done it to "follow Jesus."

There are a lot of folks who will have trouble with this one. "We are saved by faith, not works!" they will cry, and yet I fear that they have never really read the Sermon on the Mount with their hearts. It is not what we say, it is not even what we believe that matters to God. For the proof is in the pudding: it is what we *do* that matters.

God does not require perfection of you. God does not require that you be "good girls and boys" and play by the rules. God does not require sacrifice, or even that you sacrifice your critical faculties. God requires of us only this: To act justly and to do deeds of lovingkindness, whether they go unpunished or not. In the end, Jesus promises, they will most definitely be rewarded.

*Jesus, it is through your constant example*
*of kindness and compassion that we see*
*how we are to live, how we are to love God,*
*how we are to consider ourselves Christians.*
*Help us to be ever mindful of those*
*who suffer, those whom we do not see,*
*those we scorn, and help us to love them*
*even as you have loved us.*
*For it is only by so doing*
*that we can consider ourselves to be*
*your presence in the world.*
*Move our hearts to compassion,*
*and our hands to acts of lovingkindness,*
*for we ask this in the name of your*
*Community, and for its sake,*
*that we may work to bring it to fruition,*
*so that we and all peoples*
*may enjoy a life of freedom and plenty,*
*and may bask in your presence. Amen.*

*You have been told, O mortal, what is good;*
*and what does God require of you*
*but to do justice, and to love kindness,*
*and to* WALK HUMBLY *with your God?*

Micah 6:8

# Chapter Nineteen

## Walk Humbly with your God

Several years ago, while I was working for *Creation Spirituality* magazine, I had the great privilege of working with my friend Jim, a former Roman Catholic priest whose ministry to the deaf was legend in the San Francisco Archdiocese. Jim finally found that the priesthood wasn't working for him and decided that he wanted to play in a rock-n-roll band instead. So he resigned his pastorate, took up with a grunge-rock group, and got himself a story in *Rolling Stone* magazine to boot.

Jim was working at *Creation Spirituality* magazine to support himself in his early garage-rock days, and one day found himself chauffeuring me around Oakland in a highly agitated state. I should say that it was I who was in the highly agitated state, not Jim. I was worried about something that I don't even remember now, and in my distress, I just barked out orders as if I were Attila the Hun.

Finally, Jim had had enough of it. He pulled the car over and gave me what-for: "Who do you think you're talking to, John? I don't like being ordered around. I need you to treat me with respect."

I hadn't realized what I was doing. I was in my own little world, obsessed by my own worries, and my own pain. When Jim called me back to reality I was flabbergasted, truly blown away. He was absolutely right, of course, and my shame level instantly went through the roof. I apologized profusely. Jim said it was okay and started the car again. He may have forgotten the incident, but for me it was a painful and important experience of being humbled.

We don't like being humbled. Chinese etiquette is concerned almost exclusively with saving face, and Westerners aren't that crazy about losing it either. In the dog-eat-dog world that working folks find themselves in, there is already a feeling of being small and insignificant; we certainly don't welcome anything that makes us feel smaller.

This is perhaps why some religious folks have such a hard time with modern science. We already feel small enough on a planet filled with over six billion other souls. But in the last 300 years, we have felt this earth itself steadily shrinking.

We used to be the center of the universe, but now we are humbled to find that not even the sun, not even our solar system, not even our own Milky Way galaxy is the center of the universe. And we, the human race, have been humbled to find that we are not the crown of creation; that we may be just one of thousands of races in the cosmos. We used to think that we had the laws of physics at our disposal, that we could describe and predict the workings of the cosmos, from the tiniest atom to the largest of galaxies. Then the theory of general relativity came along, followed quickly by quantum mechanics, and every Newtonian rule we had about how the universe works went out the window, leaving us feeling not only small, but relatively stupid as well.

This sense of perspective (that we have only recently gained) is a tough one to swallow for those who still think we are the apple of God's eye. It is a difficult period of adjustment for the human race, one from which I believe we will emerge more mature, more realistic than we could have dreamed of before. I am an optimistic person: change is always painful; growth is always hard; but we are almost always better for it, once we go through it.

In fact I believe that our present disease, post-modernism, the system under which we live today, in which all the moorings of science and religion have been stripped away, will ultimately prove to be our salvation, once we get over the shock.

The shock is caused only because our paradigm has been upset. A paradigm is a conceptual framework into which the universe fits in such a way that we can make sense of it and function in it. The medieval paradigm of a three-tiered universe, with heaven on top, earth in the middle, and hell beneath, has been shown up as the mythology it is. We have been humbled, and it is not a pleasant experience.

Like all little boys, I loved Robin Hood. I loved the whole adventure, regardless of who was telling the story, or whether it was a movie or a cartoon. I especially loved the ending, though. If you recall, Richard the Lionheart had gone off to fight in the Crusades, leaving his weak, conniving brother, Prince John, on his throne. Prince John was a despot and Robin of Locksley operated under the malignant paradigm of John's government as best he could. But in that paradigm everything was upside down: the bad guys were in charge and the good guys were turned into the bad guys. Everything was twisted, and the land suffered.

Remember the joy, though, when King Richard returned. The twisted paradigm was gone in a puff, and the true and proper paradigm took its place. Prince John was humbled, but all the land prospered.

I submit that we have been living under the paradigm of Prince John for way too long, my friends. We have exalted to power those who would exploit the people, and the land has suffered. We have puffed ourselves up until we believed that we were the center and crown of God's creation, and we felt at liberty to destroy this creation. We prop up those who uphold our own selfish interests and demonize those who cry for justice and change. And we resist any challenge to our allegedly "divinely ordered" paradigm.

Post-modernism is God's word of truth which humbles us to the core. And Process Thought is a roadmap to life in this scary new universe. It hands us the paradigm of King Richard, a framework of right relationship in which we see ourselves as precious and integral members of a great web of being, in which we are no more or less important than any other strand in that web. It calls us to see ourselves as we really are: parts of this whole, not the summit. It calls us to right relationships with our fellow human beings: relationships of equality and mutual respect. It calls us to right relationship with our fellow creatures, relationships of interdependence and awe. It calls us to right relationship with the earth, relationships of both sustenance and reciprocity.

There are two Micahs in scripture. George Marshall writes in his wonderful book, the *Challenge of a Liberal Faith*, that it is our task to choose between them (p. 22). The first Micah we encounter in the book of Judges. This wealthy man has his own private chapel, his own gods, and even his own priest to serve the spiritual needs of his household. One day, some Israelites were passing through, demolished the chapel, stole all the gods, and offered Micah's priest a higher-paying job. No dummy, the priest went with the Israelites. The scripture says that Micah followed after them, crying "You have taken away my gods which I made, and the priest, and you are gone away: and what do I have left?"

The second Micah comes nearly a thousand years later, in a time when Israel's own house of worship has been destroyed and her people carried off into exile. This Micah, however, does not despair at having the trappings of his religion torn away. He confronts the people of Israel with a new paradigm. Religion, he tells them, is not in a building or in rituals or in gods made of stone—you have been told what true religion is: act justly, love kindness, walk humbly with your God.

Contemporary Christians have been like the first Micah, despairing that our gods have been carried away. Source criticism has done away with biblical authority and history betrays the church's claim to sole truth. Our chapel has been sacked, and we feel bereft of spiritual meaning, crying like the first Micah, "You have taken away my gods... and you are gone away: and what do I have left?" This is where we are at the turn of this century. We feel bereft, even abandoned by God. It is painful, but it will pass.

Chicken Little, take heart. The sky is not falling. That is just your paradigm in tatters at your feet. The sky is still high and hale. And though you feel humbled, be of good cheer, for you are in the company of billions of priceless and humble beings—*actual occasions*—who will make you feel welcome and needed. The new paradigm might feel scary and shaky; but that is just your legs that are shaking. You will soon learn to trust, and the ground will once again feel firm.

This shift into a healthier paradigm is already underway. Consciousness is being drawn from the mere trappings of faith to the true action of it. We are being called to move away from the outward appearances, into an interior reality. From a place of safety into a place of challenge; from a place where it is how we look that matters, into a place where it is what we *do* that matters.

Once blinded by our own worries, and our own concerns, in Process Thought we are being called back to reality, as Jim called me back justly and forcefully so many years ago. Just like that encounter, it is painful; as being humbled always is. But in it we are also being called back to health, to wholeness, and to right and true relationship.

*Wise and embracing God,*
*you are so much bigger than all of our ideas about you*
*and we have come to find*
*that most of our ideas about ourselves are wrong.*
*Comfort us in our humility, give us courage*
*to take our right and proper place in your creation*
*not as masters of each other, but as companions;*
*not as masters over other creatures, but as their equals*
*not as masters over the earth, but as daughters and sons*
*with true gratitude for our mother earth;*
*and to walk with you with humility,*
*all the days of our lives. Amen.*